COWLEY PUBLICATIONS is a ministry of the brothers of the Society of Saint John the Evangelist, a monastic order in the Episcopal Church. Our mission is to provide books and resources for those seeking spiritual and theological formation. COWLEY PUBLICATIONS is committed to developing a new generation of writers and teachers who will encourage people to think and pray in new ways about spirituality, reconciliation, and the future.

CHURCH & STAGE

CHURCH & STAGE

Producing Theater for Education, Praxis, Outreach, and Fundraising

Dean J. Seal

Cowley Publications

Cambridge, Massachusetts

Published in the United States of America by Cowley Publications, a division of the
Society of Saint John the Evangelist. No portion of this book may be reproduced,
stored in or introduced into a retrieval system, or transmitted, in any form or by any
means—including photocopying—without the prior written permission of Cowley
Publications, except in the case of brief quotations embedded in critical articles and
reviews.

Professionals and amateurs are hereby informed that the plays included in this
volume, *Three Wise Men and One Wise Guy* and *Herod and Pilate*, being fully protected
under the Copyright Laws of the United States of America and all other countries of
the Berne and Universal Copyright Conventions, are subject to a royalty. All rights
including, but not limited to, professional, amateur, recording, motion picture,
recitation, lecturing, public reading, radio, television, and internet broadcasting, and
the rights of translation into foreign languages are expressly reserved. Permission for
all such rights must be secured from the author's representatives. All inquiries
regarding these rights should be addressed to Total Creative Control, 3425 Girard
Avenue, Minneapolis, MN 55408.

Library of Congress Cataloging-in-Publication Data:

Seal, Dean J., 1955-
  Church & stage : producing theater for education, praxis, outreach, and
fundraising / Dean J. Seal.
    p. cm.
  Includes bibliographical references (p.   ).
  ISBN 1-56101-233-5 (pbk. : alk. paper)
  1. Drama in Christian education.   2. Theater—Religious aspects—Christianity.
  I. Title: Church and stage.   II. Title.
  BV1534.4.S43 2005
  246'.72–dc22

                                                              2005012072

Cover design: Brad Norr Design
Interior design and production: Andrew MacBride

This book was printed in the United States of America on acid-free paper.

Cowley Publications
4 Brattle Street
Cambridge, Massachusetts 02138
800-225-1534 • www.cowley.org

Contents

Special thanks . . .

To Tatha Wiley, Jann Cather Weaver, and
Michael Wilt, for taking my ideas and giving them
form and meaning for readers besides myself.
Merci Beaucoup.

This book is dedicated to Kirsten,
who has been with me at every stage.

CHURCH & STAGE

1 Who This Book is For and What It is About

This book is for two groups of people. It is for theater people who want to work more in churches, and it is for people in churches who want to employ theater in ministry. As a person who has worked in both worlds, I think both groups will find this book to be a handy reference.

I used to be the producer of the Minnesota Fringe Festival in Minneapolis, and it became the largest such festival in the nation. *Fringe* is a technical term for a non-juried festival; in other words, fringe festivals promote utter freedom of speech on stage. This draws a lot of people who are doing original work, and it is a good thing because, although there isn't much money around to produce new original work, some small shows are still very much worth doing.

What we did was demystify the term *producer*. Actors learned how to produce themselves instead of waiting for someone else to wave the magic wand. A producer normally lines up the cash to pay for things like advertising, salaries, sales and marketing, and glitz on stage to sell tickets. What we did at the Minnesota Fringe was teach about alternative ways to produce theater: non-cash marketing; non-advance, piece-of-the-door paychecks; and using great *ideas* to draw people to the theater instead of expensive props, sets, and costumes. Fringe attendance went from 4,400 to 28,000 in four years; recently the Minnesota Fringe hit a record attendance of 50,000.

Why all the success? Because the ideas were good, the artists were dedicated, the prices were low, and *everybody could afford to take a chance.* The audience could afford to try a few shows that they didn't know about, and performers could afford to try some ideas that were more chancy than usual. Low overhead means low risk *and* artistic freedom.

Another aspect of my experience at the Minnesota Fringe was producing shows in churches, using churches as venues. The churches were happy to have us, and not just for the moderate rents we paid. The churches were also looking for is what is called a *portal experience:* the theater production brings local people to the church that would never have come in for a worship service. It gets them in the door, and once they are there, they are free to look around, to see, to realize, "There's a church here!" At St. Mark's Episcopal Cathedral in Minneapolis an employee tells of two people who came into the church bookstore and said, "We want to buy a bunch of books about your church. We came here last Sunday—and we thought it was really great!" The employee asked, "How did you hear about St. Mark's?" and the answer was, "We came here for a show at the Fringe Festival."

Many church buildings are used only two or three days a week. And they're finding that theater is a great way to open their doors to the community and to artistic events. The shows don't have to be specifically about Jesus or typical "religious matters"—they can be shows about spirituality, about ethics. My favorite example of secular theater that belongs in a church theater setting is *All My Sons* by Arthur Miller. This modern classic is about a World War II-era businessman whose uses inadequate manufacturing practices to save money and keep the business afloat for his sons when they come home from the war. He cuts corners, however, and knowingly ships out faulty products that

cause the deaths of twenty-one test pilots. He loses more than
his business; when his sons find out, he loses them too. That's
an ethical story that has a home as much in a church as at the
Guthrie Theater, Minneapolis's premier professional theater. It
is a story of a dilemma we all potentially face when we go to work:
Are we willing to cheat somebody else to benefit our own family? Can we say that it is okay to rob people on the job so we can
feed our baby at home? These are big, central questions in any
person's life, with or without active engagement with a faith tradition.

I see a great opportunity for the development of sacred performance in any church, for any reason. There's a lot of great
material available, and it's a great way to bring people together.
Theater-goers who enjoy fringe-type performances often find
that it is easy to strike up conversations with people in line because they know in advance what they have in common: the love
of seeing live theater. There is, absolutely, a significant market
of serious theatergoers looking for cheap tickets to small theaters
that use imagination before money.

In this environment that I am describing, you see how far
you can get with no money at all. The fact is you can get *all the
way* with no money at all—for instance, by staging original adap-
tations of Bible stories using volunteer actors with no special costumes, staging, or lighting in your church's community room.
The trick is, if you are going to spend any money at all, to begin with very little investment, and see if you can make back what
you spend in ticket sales. You may break even. You might just
come out ahead. If you do, you can use that as seed money for
the next show, or it can go to a food shelf or a mission trip or a
congregation in Africa or Brazil or Montana. That's up to you
and your church. The trick is to plan out a budget, see what you
have available to you, and then leverage the resources you have
around you before laying out the cash.

But the most tangible thing that a theater program does is
bring people together in a room. Whether on stage or in the

audience, theater participants are not separated by the machinery of modern life, the isolating technologies that we all encounter daily. We sit down in front of a computer, then we get into a car, then we go home and sit in front of the TV, and pretty soon we haven't talked to *anybody* without some sort of electronic medium in between. We become distanced from what other people's lives are about. In theater you have to interact with people, you have to rehearse with them; if somebody has bad breath, you have to say, "Here's an Altoid, pal." And if the material is good, chances are you are dealing with important ethical issues, in a way you *never* will by watching "Friends" on TV.

Retired Harvard theologian Gordon Kaufmann says that after studying theology for forty years he believes the best way to envision God is that God *is* creativity; God is *serendipitous creativity.* He is the Creator. A common name for God in Native American theology and Eastern theology is *The Uncreated.* God is the only uncreated thing; everything else was created by God. The Big Bang, for instance, is one moment of creation 15 billion years ago that's still going on. We live in a serendipitously creative environment; things affect us, and we create our life. That is true of our art and of writing as well. We are presented with infinite possibilities at any given point in time, but we are finite beings, and we have to choose among these possibilities. The choice we make frequently comes about serendipitously. The notion of God being a serendipitous force of creativity makes a lot of sense.

Making art definitely requires a leap of faith. A leap of faith is *essential.* It's Kierkegaard's big idea, and now it's a country western song, but it's still true. The leap of faith is this: at a certain point, we don't know what to do, but we still have to act. In the Acts of the Apostles, Paul was becoming nervous about preaching in Corinth. "One night the Lord said to Paul in a vision, 'Do not be afraid, but speak and do not be silent; for I am with you, and no one will lay a hand on you to harm you, for there are many in this city who are my people'" (Acts 18:9–10 NRSV). This is good advice in the creative process as well. Do not fear. Let the Holy Spirit have room to participate. Don't worry about the results; just get something down on paper.

The rewards of working in the theater are not found just in awards ceremonies with little gold statues, nor in the kind of big fat paychecks received by the tiniest percentage of people in show business. The satisfaction comes from working with other people and finding the ties that bind us; in producing, performing, attending, and discussing the show. Theater is a very direct form of community where everyone is welcome. Doing theater in the church ratchets up the quality level a bit because the focus transcends commercial success; it's about the quality of the message. When we combine church and stage we take leaps of faith as a community; at the same time we open our doors to new neighbors. In the practice of theater we gain many things: community, literacy, culture, history, the powers of speech and gesture. This contributes to the better, fuller life that Jesus proclaimed: "I came that they may have life, and have it abundantly" (John 10:10 NRSV).

And that, I believe, is sacred.

2 | Church and Stage Entwined

AN OVERVIEW OF THE CONNECTIONS BETWEEN RELIGION AND THEATER

How did we get the kind of theater we have? What insights can we gain from the interaction of religious forces and theatrical forms that will help us understand what is valuable about theater to us today? In order to better understand the history of theater and its interaction with culture, we will examine the relationship between the sacred event and the theatrical moment, and develop some insight into the theatrical aspects of the church and the liturgical aspects of the theater.

These two questions come together in three periods that helped to define the theater we have today. First, the development of Greek tragedy; second, the evolution of liturgical drama into the morality plays of the Medieval period; and third, the merging of folk tales and morality plays to form the secular theater that matured in the Elizabethan age and peaked with the work of William Shakespeare. At each of these stages, the power of theater to instruct, edify, coerce, encourage, or otherwise inspire was shaped by the spiritual needs and practices of the age. Theater was for each of these times a means for people to establish community, and to give thought and action to the morals, virtues, and values of the society at large. A spiritual life has two sides: the individual's interior life and the life experienced within community. We cannot live a spiritual life in a vacuum; therefore, a society needs ways in which it can demonstrate and reinforce the values that make it what it is. Theater is a very good way to fulfill both sides of that quest for a balanced spiritual life.

The Birth of Greek Drama

There is more than one theory about how tragedy emerged from the murk of pagan Greek celebrations. Addressing this question from the point of view of the playwright helps us to understand how plays are put together. The model formulated by Gerald Else seems to me to be the most compelling and useful in this regard.

The format of Greek tragedy as we know it comes from a festival called the City Dionysia, the urban celebration of Dionysius on his feast day originally included feasting, drinking, human sacrifice, and an escalating frenzy of drunkenness and hedonism. This festival was tied into the ritual elements of celebrating the return of spring and with it, fertility, human reproduction, and successful harvests. As the society developed, the celebration began to lose some of its extreme behaviors. A contest was established in 566 B.C.E. at the Panathenaic Festival that tested the powers of performance of the Homeric epics, the *Iliad* and the *Odyssey*. The performers were called *rhapsodes,* and the contest was founded by Pisastratus, a political leader who found the tales ennobling, unifying, elevating, and entertaining. There was a great deal of tension between the ruling classes and the underclass, and Pisastratus wanted to revive a sense of "Greekness" that might overcome these differences.

Gerald Else calls the epics the "core curriculum" of heroic virtues, which include "courage, tenacity, faithfulness, courtesy, consideration, dedication of one's entire being to an overriding ideal of nobility and excellence, a dedication to something higher than one's self." These epics were performed with a chorus and a single actor. The chorus began by describing the setting and the basic story (prologue), and the actor came in and gave a set speech which elaborated the story, the action, and the consequences. The performance usually ended with a choral presentation. The actor led the chorus, directing their responses, and it was the actor who received the prize (possibly a goat, which gave rise to the term *tragedy* from *tragoidia*, or goat-singer).

The effect of these tales on the population was demonstrated by the victories of the Greeks, specifically the Athenians, over the Persians at Marathon and Salamis, when the entire population rose to the occasion and faced death in order to survive and win a victory over annihilation. These victories had a transformative effect on the population, because they now understood that they could be heroes in their own lives, that there is something immortal in everyone, and that destiny could be assaulted and changed by the determination of the individual. They became more confident in their ability to save themselves and less dependent on their gods. Consequently, the performances began to focus more on the individual and less on blind forces of nature. And as faith in the gods diminished, theater prospered.

Thespis first put this newfound sense of unity to use in the competitions in 534 B.C.E. He was the first to single out the epic hero for direct impersonation in telling these tales. Instead of acting as narrator, director, and several characters, indicated with a mask here or a prop there, he put forth a single character, the central one, and made the epic hero the focus of the event. The emphasis on the individual in storytelling underlined the distinction between the individual portrayed and the mass hysteria of the Dionysian revels. It brought the Greeks into an imaginative realm of heightened individualism, accenting a sense that maybe people were more in charge of their own destiny than the gods were. Dramatically, we see the storyteller's job move over to the chorus, who fills in details on the story and comments on the action being portrayed. The chorus becomes the cohort of the audience instead of just part of the story. This heightens the effect of a dramatic presentation by creating the *suspension of disbelief* on the part of the audience, where the actor pretends to be a part of the re-enactment of the story instead of just the teller of the story.

The contribution of Thespis results in a valuable perspective: we see the hero as the hero sees himself, we see the hero in interaction with others instead of just being told about it, and we see the hero as others see him. The hero is now perceived as a three-dimensional character.

The revolution unleashed by Thespis was more fully realized by Aeschylus. He added the second actor, which presented the hero in contrast to another and in interaction with another. He added another layer of richness to the story by increasing the intensity of focus on the decision to act, the tragic choice that the hero makes, which inevitably leads to the *pathos*, the moment of catastrophe, when he falls. Aeschylus also rearranged the organization of episodes so that the dramatic structure leads up to or away from the decision to act and the consequences of the decision.

A word needs to be said here as to why the pathos moment is so powerful to us. Athenians were fond of funerals, which are communal acts of dealing with loss, and the tragic moment is very much a communal mourning of a heroic person who has fallen. The heroic aspect of this character attracts us to the story, but the fall, mortality, and suffering of the hero connect him to our lives. There are few experiences more profound than that of the sharing of a loss of a life held dear, because it is in a very real sense a preparation for facing one's own losses and, ultimately, death. Watching the hero face his fate, we learn to face the central truth of life: it is finite, we are mortal, all is temporary. Aeschylus said that we can learn only through suffering, and by living through the hero's suffering we are ennobled. The performed tragedy gives meaning to the hero's death, thus giving meaning to his life. Meaning is something we all yearn for.

The development of Greek tragedy takes us from elaborate storytelling of a cultic nature, describing heroism in general, to the emergence of the secular hero who demonstrates the power of individual choice and its consequences. It was an enormous stride forward in humanity's perception of itself.

The Medieval Church: Miracles and Corpus Christi

The Romans accepted and expanded the model of Greek tragedy and comedy, but during an extended period after the fall of Rome, this kind of performance was almost totally abandoned. Medieval Europe witnessed the re-emergence of the theatrical form in the interaction of church, state, and populace in England. Here we will trace the forms of drama, and the political and religious issues that influenced them and led to this resurrection of tragedy.

When the Roman Empire pulled out of Britain in about 800 C.E., it left behind not just walls and aqueducts, but also performance traditions of wandering minstrels, mimes, and the rituals of the Catholic faith. The "dark ages" were marked by the maintenance of literacy only in the monasteries, which held theatrical performance in very low esteem. The tradition of Roman and Greek theater was pagan, sexual, satirical, and anti-Christian. Actors were considered to be of lower status than prostitutes, and in fact couldn't be baptized. Apart from the wayward street performer, public performance began and ended with the Church. As Christianity's power flourished, public professional theater diminished.

The essence of drama in the Church was ceremony, and each ceremony was strictly executed according to spiritual and theological precepts. The core of the service was the Sacrament of Communion. This aspect of the celebration of the Mass was unchanging. But there were also the feast days—commemorative events which were tied to specific dates in the church calendar. The Catholic fathers used these events to instruct the populace in the stories that made up the faith. A good example is Palm Sunday, when worshipers were given palms to wave. The historical records suggest that a re-enactment, including someone representing Jesus riding into Jerusalem on a colt, with robes and palm leaves spread before him and hosannas being shouted, would be performed on that day. These symbolic actions and objects were instructive in recalling the events that lie behind the Christian ritual, and were used to instruct the faithful. More involved versions were used to instruct the priests.

Owing to a number of social forces at work in about 1050, these special event performances began to gain in importance and stature. First, the monolithic grip of the Church on the populace was starting to become loosened. Second, the economy was starting to come under the sway of businessmen who formed guilds, or associations of tradesmen organized by trade, who then regulated how commerce was executed in town—usually to the point of electing the mayors and other important political figures. Third, the universities were making inroads on the Church's dominance in education, and they rapidly began to supplant the monasteries as centers of learning.

The Church was put in the position of needing to reach out to the population in new and innovative ways. The feast days, or festivals, were given greater focus, because they could involve the people in learning about the faith. A major signpost in these changes is *The Mystery Of Adam*, which emerged about 1150 as the first play known to have been performed in both Latin and the vernacular. The play told the stories of Adam and Eve, Cain and Abel, and the Prophets, the latter dramatizing the Old Testament patriarchs foretelling the coming of the Christ. The performances outgrew the interior of the church building and took place outside, usually using a wall of the church for a backdrop.

This means of telling the stories of the Bible grew in acceptance and size with the Feast of Corpus Christi, which began in 1311, and was universally accepted in the church by about 1350. In the face of creeping secularization, the spiritual goal of this festival was to emphasize the redemptive power of the bread and wine. During a time that human lives were normally short, unhappy, and brutish, Corpus Christi offered meaning through celebration of the life of Jesus, the union of the human and the divine, and the promise of redemption through Jesus' sacrifice.

The secular goal, however, was to keep the people, especially the newly independent tradesmen, involved in the church year. The plays were performed at the Corpus Christi Festival in an annual cycle, usually in the spring or summer, and the tradesmen were recruited to sponsor a specific story—for example, the bakers might sponsor the tale of the Loaves and Fishes—and they would supply the performers, props, costumes, and staging. The more elaborate events could begin with the fall of Adam and go all the way to doomsday—the end of the world—with each significant aspect of the story performed by a specific guild. The pageants also went to great lengths to create miraculous special effects. Thus were the people and the guilds involved in the productions brought to the masses in the local language.

The involvement of the guild members eventually led to their having more control of the festivals. They were less and less under the thumb of the Church. The performances began to be linked to local events, like the feast day for the patron saint of the city, and content began to be totally in the vernacular, a move away from the international scope of Latin and universal church authority.

Even content moved away from the strict telling of the Bible story to include a kind of crowd-gathering comic farce at the beginning of each episode. These comedies generally involved devils, villains, or buffoons, and exposed human failings in the light of the ideals of the church. They contrasted human failings and divine commandments, the fashionable with the eternal. They were always in part intended to teach, but they survived because they were effective theatrical entertainment. *The Second*

Shepherd's Play is a good example of an entire farce incorporated into the nativity story. The shepherds who are welcomed to the birthplace of the Christ are first nearly frozen to death, then have to chase after a stolen lamb, and are almost bamboozled by a trickster who tries to convince them that the lamb in the house is actually his very ugly child.

At the height of this type of performance, the Miracle Plays or Cycle Plays represented what had worked for Rome and Greece before: a combination of effort with church, state, and populace each playing a role. They were ceremonial, reserved for special occasions, and all-inclusive in participation. They were educational *and* entertaining. The audience could relax and enjoy, attentive to the message of the Bible story or distracted by the skit. Either way, it bound the community in a shared experience that lasted for months in its planning, rehearsal, execution, and discussion. And once the plays began to be performed in the language of the people, they became instruments of the emerging European nationalism. The essence of their success and longevity was that they were community-builders, a chance for everyone to get in the act of hands-on participation, but also to share in a moral universe, a tradition that reached into both the ancient past and the foreseeable future, into the individual's future, and into life after death.

The church dramas, as mentioned, included little farces that still dealt with the moral underpinnings of Christian philosophy. Elements of comedy were drawn from the Feast of Fools and mummer's plays. In the Feast of Fools, "usually celebrated about January first, even ordinarily pious priests and serious townsfolk donned bawdy masks, sang outrageous ditties, and generally kept the whole world awake with revelry and satire," writes Harvey Cox in his book *The Feast of Fools.* In these events, the power structure was overthrown (temporarily) and subject to ridicule. Boy bishops were appointed and authority figures were roundly mocked. People would sing out of tune, ring the church bells at inappropriate times, and use smelly objects like shoes as a censer. Mummer's plays (*momer* is a French word meaning "those who wear masks") retained a more dramatic mixture of storytelling and comedy. In mummer's plays, something miraculous could happen, like the resurrection of the dead brought about by the chicanery of a quack doctor. As these events grew more and more out of hand, the Church began to suppress them, and banned the Feast of Fools entirely by the 1500s.

One of the results of this suppression was the growth of secular farce, which combined the moralistic tone of the message of the Church with the ribald traditions of folk tales and street performing. Basic elements of the story lines described imperfect humans within the social order, displaying imperfections like marital infidelity, quarreling, cheating, and acts of hypocrisy, all delivered in a rather cynical tone; sentiment was absent. The victor in these was the clever man who lied and cheated his way to victory, without censure, over his less intelligent opponents, because the dupes were gullible and stupid and therefore deserving of their fate.

Another outgrowth of the church pageants was the morality play. Morality plays grew out of the *Pater Noster*, the prayers that dealt with the seven deadly sins and the seven cardinal virtues, told via allegory, a common means of evoking useful attributes. The plenitude of outdoor preachers who seized on these seven-and-seven subjects made them familiar to the listener; but the emerging conflict between the Roman Catholic Church and the Anglican Church, begun by Henry VIII in 1534, made the morality play a useful form of proselytizing as each side jockeyed for the hearts and minds of the English population. Morality plays were expressions of dogma and were taken very seriously as means of instruction and evangelization.

The best-known morality play is probably *Everyman*, in which the hero is informed that he is about to be summoned to death. He searches for a companion to accompany him on his long journey, but finds that Friendship, Beauty, Goods, and assorted worldly attributes will not come with him; only Good Deeds will follow him into the grave. Another is *King John*, which combined historical and allegorical figures, and became a precursor to Shakespeare's chronicle, or history, plays.

At the same time that forms of theater were becoming more varied, the same burghers who had given substance to the cycles were now hiring actors to create interludes, or small entertainments to go between dances and singing. In the same way that mimes were recruited for the cycles, so actors were recruited out of them, diversifying performance capabilities and enriching opportunity for the people who produced secular performance.

As we approach the Golden Age of English Theater, we see that the form of cycle and pageant plays had very gradually become sophisticated enough that people wanted more. While these performance forms worked well to hold a community together in thought, word, and deed, they were about to undergo the same stresses as the rest of the community when questions of royal succession became entangled in the Reformation. The performances had outgrown the Church, physically and metaphorically, and under the guise of the morality plays, theater began to re-emerge. But it took political interference of considerable magnitude to set the stage for the English theatrical renaissance of the late 1500s.

Elizabeth I and the Consolidation of Royal Power

The story of theater in London in the sixteenth century is the story of Elizabeth I and her nerve-racking rise to power. After spending her early years in constant danger of being executed by one faction or another, Elizabeth gradually exerted so much power that by the time James I came to London to take her place after her death in 1603, she had built what amounted to an absolute monarchy. Part of this control was control over what people saw and heard on the stage. Elizabeth helped forge a new path for secular theater in her efforts to reduce the religious conflict in her nation, and it opened new possibilities for the secular theater.

Elizabeth's father, Henry VIII, had set the stage for Elizabeth in a number of ways. First, he pulled England out of the Roman Catholic Church and named himself the head of the Anglican Church. This effectively made religious disagreements with him treasonable, and a capital offense. Though Mary I tried to bring Catholicism back during her reign after Henry, the precedent was there; the regent of Britain would rule over the church too.

Second, Henry was a big fan of big entertainments, and consolidated the business of live performance in his time by regulating it and creating the post of Master of Revels. He recognized that many noblemen kept companies of actors and performers for various times of the year, and that these companies wandered freely, seeking to mount performances in out-of-the-way towns and villages, when not employed by the nobles. Local administrators found these performers to be disruptive. They distracted people from work and worship and generally created havoc through their itinerant lifestyle. So Henry required that actors be licensed to someone of noble blood, and held that person responsible for the actions of his actors. Though this limited the freedom of the actors and reduced the number of acting companies on the road, it also legalized the actor and made acting an activity approved and supported by the Crown.

Elizabeth took this one step further, as she did with many issues of authority. She licensed all acting troupes to the Crown itself. In this way, Elizabeth not only had the authority to approve acting troupes, she could also exert critical control over the content of what was being performed. Theater was coming under extensive criticism from the Protestants and Anglicans, who found it to be too Roman (in both pagan and Catholic senses of the word). The opposite view was maintained by theater's defenders, notably Sir Philip Sidney, who argued in his *Defense of Poesey* (1553) that "Literature is the most effective of all human

works in teaching morality and moving men to virtuous action."
Sidney's work had a strong influence on Ben Jonson and, some
surmise, Shakespeare.

Elizabeth decided to render the point moot by exerting her
critical control over the stage. In 1559, as one of her first acts
upon ascension, she banned the performance of any plays that
discussed religious or political subjects of the day. Stories from
the past may have political content, or may include religious matters or characters related to the Church; but they could not be
about the politics then consuming the court. This brought an
end to the production in Britain of the medieval morality plays,
because they were used to propagate Roman Catholic dogma.

This had two enormous effects on performing. First, it de-
prived the theater of its religious and social function, and forced
it to exist on purely commercial and artistic terms. So while
drama was made secular, it remained committed to a mission
of imbuing a moral effect on the audience and exhibiting a moral
force in the universe. The second effect was to create a great
deal of interest in early Greek and Roman work, which had
been preserved by the Spanish Moors and re-circulated into European centers of learning. This was seen as work that could be
presented within the context of Elizabeth's constraints. None
of it was Christian, and nothing ancient could have any bearing
on what was happening in the present. Could it?

The Queen attended a performance of *Gorboduc,* written by
two students named Thomas Sackville and Thomas Norton.
Gorbuduc was the first English tragedy written in the classic tradition, and followed in the tradition of the 1516 morality play
Magnificence, which described the lifestyle appropriate to a ruler.
The play stressed the dangers of leaving an uncertain succession behind. While the play itself was not significant in form,
the Queen understood the theater as a means of teaching and
of conveying behavioral preferences; she also saw that it could
become a medium by which her will could be supported in another arena. After this, interest in plays about English history

and plot lines lifted from old Greek and Roman plays were acceptable and sought after. This is especially evident in the works of Shakespeare.

Plays changed in a number of significant ways in this period. The changes that are pertinent to our topic are as follows, summarized from Oscar Brockett's *History of Theater.*

The plays are shaped by a notion of moral order under which humans are free to make choices, but are ultimately accountable to forces greater than themselves. Though characters are still caught in a battle between good and evil, the portrayal of the conflict is much less obvious than in medieval drama. Moral tone is established through poetic imagery, soliloquies, maxims, and proverbs.

Playwrights flourished in both state-supported theaters and in public commercial houses for many years, until the death of Elizabeth. King James I was more like Henry VIII in his love for revels. He ascended to the throne in 1603, a year historians date as the time when masques and spectacles became more important. In 1604 he licensed all performing troupes to the Stuart family. In 1608 he became enraged at a performance of a play with political content, and ordered the offending troupe disbanded. Significant playwriting fell off beginning about 1610—no wonder—and James's taste for masques and spectacles was indulged by Ben Jonson and many others under the financial sway of his authority. The masques became competitive, were referred to as "The Theater of Power" and "The Politics of Spectacle," and soon became demonstrations of wealth and fealty, no longer instructing or probing the decisions of the monarch.

But while Elizabeth reigned, something special had happened in English theater. With religion and politics eliminated as subject matter, the theater had to rethink itself. It had to avoid current events and dig deeply into history; it had to ignore current tradition and dig deeply into plays from the past; it had to focus on bringing new skills and new craftsmanship to the telling of tales, as the customary forms had been forbidden. And, as in

everyother European country, England was developing a nation-
alistic consciousness through its language, which was expedited
by the printing press, and developing a national identity with
the aid of the performing arts. So while a new identity of nationalism was being born, the old identity of international Chris-
tendom was fading. As the nature of community changed, the
stage was forced to change with it, and this change forced new
light into the theoretical aspects of creating theater. It was a ripe
and fulsome time, diminished by King James and King Charles
after him, and snuffed by the Puritans in 1642, when they closed
all the theaters.

3   How the Arts Can Enhance the Spiritual Life

The power of great art is undeniable. Its ability to reach out and grab the viewer's undivided attention for hours on end is unique in the human experience. In a class I took with Wilson Yates, he talked about how great religious art "pulls us onto sacred ground." That is, the mere viewing of an evocative painting can transform everyday moments into something deeper and more meaningful. It can leap across space and time to give body to our spirituality and begin a deep conversation, with us and for us, about what we believe and why we believe it.

In his article "Intersections of Art and Religion," Yates offers a lucid commentary on the ways in which powerful art can aid in the conveyance of spiritual meaning when properly used in a religious setting, and offers five examples of intersections between art and the spiritual life of the congregation.

Art has a role in religious ritual. The role of the arts in religious ritual is manifest in familiar physical elements (the architecture of a religious space, music, stained glass, fabrics, sculpture, painting); the physical process of the rituals of the service (standing, sitting, kneeling, processing); and the spoken arts (readings from the scriptural text and poetry, the sermon, prayer, and even the announcements). When these are done with care and intentionality they add a deeper dimension to their content.

Yates says, "We begin to see how works of art become significa n t forms [forms that signify], become significant means through which a people enter into the realm of religious experience."

Art raises religious questions about the meaning and purpose of life.   A powerful painting, for example, can isolate a tragic moment and bring sharp focus to an act of violence, the pain of someone wronged. Art, says Yates, "can engage us in recognizing and responding to matter of ultimate significance, matters related to birth and death, order and chaos, being and nothingness, love and hate, alienation and wholeness, the demonic and the divine."

Art reveals the character of a historic faith.   This is evident in an abundance of examples: Mozart's Requiem, the poetry of the Psalms, old Negro spirituals, stained-glass windows at Chartres, whether experienced in or out of the context of worship, signify a community and its culture.

Art is prophetic in its judgment of idolatry and injustice. Yates describes a sculpture by Henry Moore, *Warrior with Shield,* which depicts a soldier who has lost both legs and his left arm; he has only his right arm with which to defend himself. Yates's interpretation demonstrates the powerfully prophetic role of art in questioning and judging idolatry and injustice: "Moore is . . . prophetic in his statement about the horror of war, of the last moment before death in battle, of the limits of defense in the face of the destructiveness of war . . . He holds his shield in one last gesture which can do nothing more than glance away one blow before the final pierce of death. His face . . . stares out toward the force of evil that is about to destroy him. The last breath is sucked in; the moment holds only futility. This is, I believe, Moore's protest against the awfulness of war's destruction. It is a strong prophetic judgment on our human idolatry and our capacity as a human community to visit destruction on our lives."

Art may become sacramental in its power; it may become the means through which divine truth and grace are mediated. Yates says, "Art may become that through which we experience the holy. Again and again, it is the burning bush that turns common ground into sacred ground and when it does so, our spirituality is nurtured." He uses the example of a painting by Marc Chagall, *The Poet with the Birds*, to demonstrate the sacred elements in a work that is not specifically spiritual: "Chagall creates a world imbued with fantasy scenes in which he weaves animals, lovers, communities, nature, and above all relationships into a fabric in which safety, love, delight, peace reign in our lives. . . . His are canvases of sacramental possibilities. His love for his wife Bela defies gravity in a burst of joy; his bouquets of flowers celebrate creation and nurture lovers; his flying fish often play violins . . . and his village lies quietly blanketed with a sense of well-being."

AND NOW, LADIES AND GENTLEMEN, THE SPIRITUAL ARTS GO TO THE THEATER

Effective art is a key ingredient of ritual; it is that which pulls us into the experience. It may be manifest in the visual setting that the architect presents, or the choreography of processing, standing, sitting, and kneeling together.

The strongest element of ritual in my experience, for example, is the shared experience of singing together, the joy and reverence that can be communicated through a powerful piece of music. This comes out of the long tradition of word-based worship in my Lutheran upbringing. The Lutheran tradition, in differentiating itself from sensibilities considered too Catholic, is almost austere in regard to church décor and antiseptic in its aversion to painting and sculpture. It is not, however, austere with its use of music.

An effective array of artistic elements, Yates says, "is the catalyst that can release in us powerful moments of recognition and identification, absorption and transcendence in which we become one with the work's representation."

T. S. Eliot comments similarly on "Music heard so deeply that you become the music while the music lasts." As my Lutheran experience confirms, music is the most successfully utilized medium for immersing the worshiper in the ritual experience. Depending on theological preferences of the denomination, other art forms have been utilized more unevenly, and in this they have missed out on real opportunity.

What is true of music, the spoken word, paintings, and sculpture in the worship service is also true of theater. Theater is all about setting up and delivering a specific *moment* when a key understanding is arrived at, or something is said, or something dramatic occurs. When it works, the audience is drawn in and experiences the same emotional impact as the character. When it works in a piece of art, the viewer is drawn into the experience that the artist is attempting to convey; and this can be a deep insight into spiritual matters.

But when it works as a part of a religious service, the art can achieve its full potential of drawing a community together. The shared experience of singing together is expanded by praying together, a deeply personal and spiritual event; or by sharing communion, the basic human experience of breaking bread together, compounded by the remembrance ritual Jesus called for the night before his execution; or by declaring a common faith and common mission that unify us on a level not found in the daily mercantile striving for the rest of our lives. The community then moves out for coffee and bakery goodies, to share stories of the week, ask after one another's health, and do all the things that a community used to do before cars and radios and telephones and computers succeeded in isolating us from one another. A community that comes together regularly has a lifesaving ability to refresh and reconnect people by giving them a chance to share their problems, joys, and pains. The common ground they find together in an effective worship service gives them immediate access to one another and enables them to trust and give and become willing to receive help from people they barely know, because they understand community to be of the very fabric of their being.

It is perhaps natural to respond to liturgical needs by attempting to bring culture into the liturgy. But experiments in this regard often go wrong. Aidan Kavanaugh, in *Elements of Rite*, hits a key concept in understanding the context of the service. "Adapting liturgy to culture invariably results in the liturgy's demise. Adapting culture to liturgy is the only alternative, a far more demanding endeavor . . . liturgy must not chase after and lend support to cultural trends." Kavanaugh's point is that he views the extant liturgy to be the focal point of our lives. He would prefer that we adapt ourselves and our lives to what we find in the historical roots of worship, rather than try to adapt what we do in the chancel to the latest fashion. We must adapt ourselves, and the culture in which we live, to the structures of meaning and expression that we find in our faith traditions. While many find newer, experimental forms to be meaningful, others experience a deep satisfaction in returning to traditional forms that date back to the Early Church. If ancient forms are recast and rethought in the light of modern sensibilities so that the effect is genuinely spiritual, then the effort to restore intentionality to a formerly rote practice can breathe new life into old forms.

My own experience is that the leaders of, for example, a "celebration service" try to generate sing-alongs with songs that no one knows, and they devolve into concerts because they are trying to play new, unfamiliar music that doesn't involve the congregation. The congregation feels like it is seeing something new, but it isn't being touched or reached. A positive experience in a celebration service results from the use of multimedia screens to give people song lyrics, which gets their noses out of the hymn book and into the open air of the sanctuary, more accessible to one another and to the mood of the room. Sing-along verses aren't about the skill of the composer, but are about bringing people into the shared worship experience. A more relaxed atmosphere is a welcome change for those who find older European traditions to be stifling or sad. Some people can only have a negative association with services that remind them of unpleasant experiences in the church of their youth, and in that case a stripped-down and energetic celebration can be refreshing, helpful, and meaningful.

The same argument comes to mind when people talk about television and radio ministries. If what they are doing is adding to our experience in a church, then maybe it's accomplishing something. But these events will never create a community via an isolating technology. The promise that "we are reaching people that wouldn't otherwise be reached" falls short of the truth by my analysis, because no one is being reached. They are hearing something outside the community-based context in which is was meant to be communicated. It's like reading one of Jesus' parables to a group of people without introducing it as a parable; they hear the narrative as a literal event rather than as a story with a different sort of meaning. They lose ground in regard to understanding and spirituality. Broadcast religious services are a viable alternative for those who are housebound or incapacitated (and who therefore need the community to come to them in human form as well); the rest of us need to get out of the house and go to church.

"The work of authentic Christian liturgy," Kavanaugh says, "requires us to employ the arts and engage in symbolic actions with the primary intention of *gathering* in the name and promise of God's self-giving incarnate act. Without the anchors of the shared teachings of Jesus, the wisdom literature, shared significant forms . . . we drift into mere cultural self-expression" (emphasis added). This is an especially dangerous temptation in the United States, which is all about self-expression, independent thought, distrust of European traditions that are seen as imperialist, and physical mobility, while at the same time loaded with a rich, diverse cultural heritage that invites experimentation of all kinds.

One of the successful experiments I have seen was when Westminster Presbyterian, my home congregation, gave the service to some of the members who are from Cameroon, and had a West African service that was drawn from both the West African Presbyterian service and from the regular lineup at Westminster. It was invigorating in that we got to hear our European traditions though another language and another rhythm. Nothing about it was strange, and nothing about it was familiar.

Finally, Kavanaugh offers advice as to where to dig for new forms when you do want to experiment. *Consumerist culture* feeds on ever-changing media hype, whereas *deep culture* is embedded in a community's history of pain and joy. The latter can maintain its power and authority if utilized carefully in a worship setting. When a community seeks to bring culture and liturgy together, it is to *deep culture* that it should turn.

Another reading on the subject, Paul Hoon's *Integrity of Worship*, proposes five directions of liturgical communication, six elements of worship, and three levels of participation. I have no problem when someone is trying to quantify the infinite; as he puts it, "understanding Christian liturgy . . . faces us with the paradoxical fusion of divine grace and human means." Without detailing all of his lists, I want to address the last item, the three levels of participation, because again I feel that the essential element in the liturgy is the sense of participation, of community interaction, the sense that the congregation feels it is surely a part of the sacred event taking place in its midst. That is the core of intentionality, which means making sure you are including the elements of worship on purpose, instead of by habit. It requires examination, discussion, and re-approval of the specific elements of worship before continuing on with them. Make sure everything has a meaning you can describe and that almost anyone can understand.

Hoon describes the three levels as: First, what the liturgy presents on the surface. Second, the consciousness of maturing into what it means to be in solidarity with the living and the dead, and with the whole people that God desires. And third, participation in the very life of God. "A sense of the divine mystery not as a puzzle to be solved, but as a wonder and a grace to live 'into.' "

The last one is a key concept because it is the experience of the presence of God that makes the event a sacred ceremony. Here is where Jesus said, "where two or three are gathered in my name, I am there among them" (Matthew 18:20 NRSV). It is here that we feel the Holy Spirit move through us as a body, as a common sense of who we are, a connection to Christians throughout the generations before us, with the hope for generations after us, that we can maintain this connection by gathering together (*to gather*) to act as one as the Body of Christ. And it is this sense that participation on an ongoing basis will be an anchor for my life, that it is there for me at the appointed time on the Sabbath, that gives hope during the madness of everyday reality, reminding me that peace is at hand.

This is something to consider when you are preparing to put together a piece of Church Theater. Done well, you are preparing a sacred ceremony. You can utilize the elements of instruction, inspiration and the combining of effect to reach into the heart of the audience, and offer them the opportunity to change. You can take a piece of wisdom that is inherent in the work you are portraying, and plant it in the heart of the people gathered in front of you as witnesses. It's a big opportunity, and a huge trust.

4 | Dr. King Would Approve

THE THEOLOGIAN ONSTAGE

The life and work of Dr. Martin Luther King, Jr. is an inspiring example of how someone lived out the life of faith in his work. It is valuable to understand that the work being described in this book isn't recommended simply because it is valuable as a means of keeping a congregation involved and busy. It is valuable because it is a means by which the process of reconciliation can be advanced, one church at a time; or one show at a time. It is not to encourage people to make theater for its own sake, but to make theater because the making of theater creates community, builds reconciliation, and involves the participants in the struggle for the betterment of the common good. It is a means by which we may live out our faith.

In his book *King Among the Theologians*, Noel Leo Erskine lays out how he sees the life of Dr. King as modeling for us the marks of the theologian. The four examples he uses are not in the context of church theater, but can be applied to it. This will be demonstrated by placing in conversation the work of Dr. King and the work of performing a Christmas mummer's play, *Three Wise Men and One Wise Guy*, at Grace-Trinity Church in Minneapolis. (The script of this play is included in appendix A.)

The play was created to be performed, in the context of the

church service, on the last Sunday before Christmas. It is only twenty minutes in length, but the process of producing it was as important as the content that was being produced, and process carries through from this show to any other.

A quick recap of the show will suffice to illustrate it.

The performance opens with a processional of the characters from the back of the sanctuary to the chancel. The *Hodie* from Benjamin Britten's *Ceremony of Carols* is being sung by a choir, which leads. The tonic note of the chord is being tolled by a handbell once per measure. Matthew and Luke (the two Gospel writers) enter, along with Herod, the Innkeeper, Mary, Joseph, the Three Wise Men, and various shepherds and sheep. The Three Wise Men in this play are Dietrich Bonhoeffer, Martin Luther King, and Mohandas Gandhi. They are wearing big masks to show who they are portraying. While the mood of the actors is serious as they arrive, the sheep are doing a soft "baa-a-a-a" to give the presentation a comedic undertone.

When all are assembled, Luke begins reading his Christmas story, and introduces the segment where Joseph and Mary are looking for a place to stay. Mary is portrayed as a woman *in extremis*, ready to give birth at any moment, and also as the Jewish mother who will never suffer in silence. After they find a place, Matthew begins narrating his part of the story, beginning with when the Three Wise Men come to Herod looking for the child. Herod instructs them to bring word back when they do locate him. When they find Mary, they offer their gifts; but Mary is irritated. She comments, "If you had been Three Wise Women, you would've got here before the baby was born! You would have brought something to eat, and some clean linens so I could change the baby. Did any of you stop to ask directions?" The Wise Men are ashamed to admit that they did not. They leave to find Mary some food.

Then the story shifts to the Shepherds being told by an angel where to look for the child. After they go looking, the Three Wise Men re-enter with Jack Finnegan, the caterer. He sings a song about how he loves to celebrate Christmas because of all the food and drink and partying; the birth of Jesus doesn't come up.

The Wise Men ask Jack why he is celebrating; Jack's lame answer is that it is the baby's birthday. Each of the Wise Men then explains what it is about the life and teachings of Jesus that they are celebrating. Jack is taught who this baby is and why we are celebrating, and then is encouraged to go back to celebration but with the intentionality of acknowledging who it is that is being celebrated; *intentionality* meaning that everything you do, you do on purpose and not because you've always done it that way or you don't know any other way.

The sheep and shepherds arrive, and they exclaim their great joy. Dr. King has a dream ("Not that one. Another one") that tells him to not go back to Herod; and everyone begins to celebrate by singing "Joy to the World." The End.

We can compare the work and the message of this play with the essential attributes of a theologian displayed in the person of Dr. King:

1. *The theologian must work from within the struggle (the struggle of oppressed people) to relate Christian faith to the concrete conditions that effect both body and soul.* The content of the play deals directly with the problem of consumerism and gluttony overshadowing the sacred elements of Christianity. Jack Finnegan is so good at the "how" of Christmas that he has forgotten the "why." As Johnson said, "Men more frequently require to be reminded than informed." In the play, the Three Wise Men do the reminding for us all.

In producing the play, we are also directly engaged in the struggle to give meaningful participation to the teenagers of the congregation, for whom the church experience is all too often either too distant and boring, or dumbed-down and pedantic. Rev. Scott Stapleton of Grace-Trinity advised that we not fear challenging the teens: "If you don't ever challenge them, they're not going to get it." Engaging them in this process helps them develop their sense of self, gives them a chance to interact meaningfully with their peers and with other members of the congregation, and gives them the challenge of taking responsibility in a communal enterprise.

In this production, the mummer's play also presents Dietrich Bonhoeffer as a minister fighting the Nazis, which is cool; the idea of a minister fighting the Nazis can appeal to teenagers in a very dramatic way, in contrast to the reserved and dignified preconception they may have of ministers from their own experience. While many are aware of Bonhoeffer and his work, many more are not, as compared to Dr. King or to Gandhi. For audience and participants alike, this is an opportunity to become exposed to a very recent and always relevant hero of the faith.

The play also provides some context for Dr. King. They may have heard about him for years, but may not have had any contact with any of his ideas apart from his most famous and often quoted "I Have a Dream" speech, given from the steps of the Lincoln Memorial. An audience has some recognition of Dr. King as a social leader, but it is easy to forget that he was also a minister, and beyond that many have never encountered him as a theologian. To put Dr. King outside of his context of activism may stimulate some new interest in him.

Finally, they learn that there are interfaith applications of Christianity through Gandhi. Gandhi is not a Christian, and in fact makes a scathing comment about Christians in the play, a comment that comes from real life ("I might have become a Christian if I hadn't met so many of them"). Yet it is news to many that Gandhi got a great deal of inspiration from Jesus. The demonstration of interfaith respect among the King, Bonhoeffer, and Gandhi characters is instructive for those who presume that we must always be on our guard with members of other faith traditions.

Also, outside of what this means to the teenaged participants, there are other messages that bubble under the surface of the text. The section where Mary chews out the Wise Men for being late and not bringing food is a gentle jab at the lack of attention to the contributions that women made to the ministry of Jesus, and how the history of Christianity might have been different, had the input of the women disciples been more widely acknowledged in the early centuries of the church. But the main point of this portrayal of Mary is to move her away from a mystical, pietistic presence and into the real world of giving birth. No matter how we interpret the stories of the conception of Jesus, he was born of a woman under difficult circumstances; it can never hurt to emphasize the very human beginning of the life of Jesus.

Mary also has a number of punch lines right in a row, which again allows us to take some biblical figures off pedestals, and relate more closely to them as humans. But the stage instructions that make her into more of a standard-issue Jewish mom, a persona developed by American Jewish comedians, give us an underlying reminder that Jesus was a Jew. His Jewishness is de-emphasized in other contexts; here is a comedic way to emphasize it.

One drawback of the script as written is that there are few roles other than Mary for women. One should feel free to cross-cast and take women actors in the roles of men whenever a surplus of female talent is available and men are scarce. The Innkeeper, Jack Finnegan, and the Shepherds could easily be played by women; the Wise Men are more of a problem. But the convention of casting a woman in a man's role seems much more readily accepted by audiences than that of casting a man in the role of a woman.

2. *The theologian must be committed to the struggle to change the world as well as willing to lay down his or her life in the quest for justice for the oppressed.* This means that the concrete problems of the community must become grist for the theological mill. Issues of economic, social, and political justice, poverty, and powerlessness must be brought from the periphery to the center of theological attention.

In content, *Three Wise Men and One Wise Guy* addresses how three prominent individuals—Bonhoeffer, Gandhi, and King—chose to follow Jesus and put their lives on the line for their cause. The fact that King died while participating in the strike of sanitation workers in Memphis amplifies the essence of the struggle and its price. It helps to define the struggle when we remember the cause that brought Dr. King to Memphis in the first place. The script also emphasizes that this type of dedication is the ultimate price of servanthood anywhere in the world.

The actor playing this role steps into the shoes of a man who is advocating love of neighbor, and can experience the connection King feels between what he knows about Jesus and how he is living his own life. It should bring into sharper focus the religious underpinnings of King's work.

The content of the play also addresses a serious problem in contemporary life, that of materialism. Materialism leads people to work too much, drink too much, spend time away from the family, and otherwise prevent connection because of a cultural emphasis on economic goals. The frenzy of Christmas shopping has disconnected people from the personhood of the Christ to the point where in many instances the two have no connection whatsoever. And there are few ideas farther out of the mainstream than one that advocates working less, spending less, and living more slowly. The message of this play is that the Christian way of life is purely countercultural to the American way of life.

3. *Reconciliation becomes the main key in which theology is set.* In describing this aspect of King's theology, Erskine uses the word *key* in two different ways. In comparing King to the work of theologian James Cone, Erskine says, "Cone postulates liberation as the main key that unlocks Scripture and at the same time provides the frame of reference for social criticism; for King, the key is reconciliation. The theme of reconciliation is the main key in which the struggle for freedom is cast."

Reconciliation is indeed the key to this work. Dr. King's

statement "Love the racist" directly echoes Jesus' command to "Love your enemy." On the surface, the Wise Men are trying to reconcile Jack's celebration with the reason for celebration. They try to raise his consciousness about what the celebration is about. In our own time, this effort is mirrored between those who take the religious aspect of Christmas very seriously and are highly critical of those who want to liven up the celebration; and those who take the celebration seriously and are highly critical of the sourpusses who want to dampen things down. The Wise Men themselves are reconciled to each other despite divergent backgrounds. The Innkeeper and his customers (Mary and Joseph) are reconciled when the Innkeeper lets them have the stable at no charge. Jack is reconciled when he learns more about who it is he is celebrating, but is still encouraged to actively spread joy throughout the community.

The presence of Gandhi reminds us that the Mahatma died in the struggle for interfaith reconciliation. His efforts to reconcile Hindus and Muslims in India was welcomed as well as met by resistance, and he was assassinated by a fellow Hindu who believed Gandhi was being too accommodating.

The Wise Men are reconciled to each other as they come in; they reconcile with Jack and Jack's family (us) in the process; and the audience/congregation is reconciled symbolically in the singing of "Joy to the World." The experience of communal hymn singing is a core production value of a service—singing together is an activity that creates community through a blending of diverse voices with a common goal. In this way, the show ends with everyone "feeling as one."

4. *Faith and* praxis—*the practice of the church*—*are conjoined as the gospel of Jesus is related to the plight of those who suffer and are heavy laden.* Erskine is focusing here on King's motivation to do more than just preach, but also to take action. Faith in this context is about having a religious belief, while praxis is the practice of faith that comes from those beliefs. Faith and praxis go hand in hand. What good is a fully developed theology when

the poor are trampled and the helpless are suffering? Erskine says, "King was not . . . overly concerned about method in theology for the sake of articulating a theological system. He allowed theology to serve the needs of the church and to provide the basis for leading oppressed people out of bondage."

In the context of church and stage, the community takes action in putting together a play. The play has content that reflects the values that we find in the Bible, especially the social gospel of Jesus. In Bonhoeffer, King, and Gandhi, we meet people who would find their lives in losing them; people who gave their lives for the sake of their friends; people who spoke in the prophetic voice that was intended to free those who are oppressed, enslaved, impoverished, hated. The play focuses our attention on people near to our own time in history who have taken the words of Jesus and turned them into action, demonstrating that what Jesus said and did is still inspiring no matter how long ago he spoke those words and performed those deeds.

The praxis of the small church in which the play was performed as a pageant and chancel drama is exemplified in the amount of time, energy, and resources it dedicates to the young people entrusted to their care. There are no priorities that are given more attention than the effort to engage and educate the youth of the church. This project came about as a means to increase the involvement of teenagers in the life of the faith; this church felt the need to specifically dedicate themselves to that task.

Bringing Dr. King into the sanctuary is worth the effort at any time, but the fact that King has a role in this play may disguise the fact that the play itself is an effort to live up to his highest ideals. This type of work is effective even if Dr. King were not in the show. Its effect comes from challenging the congregation and its youth to take on the assignment and execute it correctly; from engaging the community and inviting their participation; from accepting the risk that it may not work or that the congregation isn't ready; and in the forthright declaration of a preferential option for the poor and oppressed lived out in the daily life of the church.

The congregation creates the community of people who put on the play. The play-giving community creates the play-going community that comes to the performance or service. That entire community is changed by the experience. They go out and affect their community at large. They may come back and join the church community, or they may not. But for the time they spent with this production, there was a community created where before there was none. Community-building is at the heart of the effort of reconciliation. And it is the essential product that theater must create, every time. Either that, or the art form fails to live up to its potential.

5   Opening the House

BRINGING THEATER
INTO THE CHURCH SPACE

There are ways to engage the process of opening up the church to the benefits of the performing arts without having to mount a show. It can be done with partnerships with existing performance organizations. Some churches rent space to theater groups for rehearsal; some rent space to theater groups for shows; some rent out their classrooms to theater schools; and some even form partnerships to share the load of maintaining a building. In this process, you open up the church to new ideas, new people, new expertise, a heightened visibility, and a new income stream.

There are two key elements that define the workability of this kind of cooperation. First, arts organizations and churches both have the greater good of the community in mind. So no matter what the religious beliefs of the artists, nor what art forms the churches know and appreciate, artists and churches generally find a way to get along. There is a mutual respect inherent in the work.

Second, theater companies and churches do not have scheduling conflicts. Theater companies rehearse during the week, performing on Friday and Saturday nights. Churches have services Sunday mornings, and often only need space on Wednesday nights for church suppers. You can both use the building only when you need to and let the other partner share the burden of overhead for the times when you are not using it.

Rentals

Churches can rent out their space to theater groups. The first advantage is that most theater groups are looking for a space when churches are not in use. They are typically looking at Friday and Saturday nights for performing and evenings for rehearsing. They are accustomed to paying for the use of space, so they have no trouble with the nominal fees that churches usually charge for rehearsal space.

What kind of large space can your church offer? Many churches have community rooms for the coffee hour and other meetings and gatherings. Some have stages and portable seating. Any sort of space is usable to the right group and the right show. The choir room, the second chapel, the youth room, whatever you have, theater people can probably make a theater out of it. A theater company could come in and use it as is, or it can bring in a small and portable lighting system. Scenery can be designed to be set up and taken down easily.

In 2005 dollars, $10 an hour is a reasonable fee for rehearsal rooms during the week and on weekends. You can charge $50 per show for bigger spaces on Friday and Saturday nights. Talk to the groups and find out what they are used to paying, and try to be cheaper than the alternatives. You are not depending on this revenue to keep the doors open, but it could develop into a significant flow of new cash (one church with which I have been associated takes in about $1,000 a month in rental income). Charge enough to cover the time it takes to manage the paperwork, but make it easy for the theater company to make money, so that they come back again and bring a steady stream of new faces through the door.

Make sure that you notify your insurance broker about the

use of the space in this way. In the unlikely event that something goes wrong, you want to be covered. Theater people tend to be rather civilized. They do not create trouble, or break things on purpose, or pick fights. You'll want to consult with your insurance agent, but a fair starting place for an insurance premium is around one dollar for each ticket sold. If your insurance person can't help you with this, call a few theaters and find the name of their broker, and go with that company. Alternatively, you can require that the theater company take out performance insurance. This is a standard requirement of theaters who provide space to different companies, and you may be able to assist the company through your own insurance agent. The key is to make sure you are protected in the event of a problem.

There is an improvisational comedy company in a church on the Upper East Side of Manhattan called Chicago City Limits. They perform on Friday and Saturday nights and teach classes and workshops during the week. On performance days, they have a big flag outside the church. It's a church basement with a stage. They got one good review in the *New York Times*, and they've run it in their advertising ever since. They had been there eleven years when I found them. That's a rental that became a small but steady partnership that creates an income stream for the church that does not depend on the response to the last sermon.

Something More Permanent: Partnerships

A very successful partnership in a very big way is the one at Old Cambridge Baptist Church (OCBC) in Cambridge, Massachusetts. OCBC is so close to Harvard Yard that it rents parking space to people going to events there. The church is listed on the National Registry of Historic Places as an outstanding example of the American gothic revival style. It was designed by Alexander R. Esty, a famed Boston architect, and built from 1867 to 1870. Members point out specific highlights with pride:

soaring ceilings, graceful arches, expansive interiors, and a great collection of stained glass including a piece attributed to Charles Lewis Tiffany of Tiffany Glass fame.

OCBC's small congregation is deeply involved in social-action issues. A cursory summary of some activities includes the following areas of participation: Massachusetts Interfaith Alliance, Greater Boston Interfaith Organization, Religious Coalition for the Freedom to Marry, the re-granting of about $2,500 to other charitable organizations, and Project Manna, to name just a few.

In 2000, OCBC's attendance was 15 to 25 people per Sunday. The church did not feel a need to become bigger for the sake of bigness. The congregation liked the warmth and familiarity of a small church. But the building had been the subject of deferred maintenance for many years. It's the largest cut-stone church in the Boston area, and has specific needs for upkeep, but lacked a financial base committed to upkeep. As more leaks and more water damage made it painfully clear, they would have to find some resources or the building would become unsafe.

At the same time, the Jose Mateo Ballet Theater was looking for a home. They had funding for a building project but wanted to be in an urban setting, which would require a larger investment than they could afford. By teaming up with OCBC, the ballet company found a home that is accessible to their audience, is perfect for its bread-and-butter teaching practice, and is a gorgeous, innovative place to stage ballet. OCBC found a financial resource from outside the church to keep its historical building intact, symbolizing their continuity with the community. As the partnership developed, there were some surprises, most of them pleasant.

Six-and-a-half days a week, Ballet Theater's dancers, teachers, musicians, and students, ranging in age from 3 to 80, fill the sanctuary (which they call Studio One), the parish hall (Studio 2), and the choir room (Studio 3) with music and movement.

On Sunday mornings, the congregation uses the same spaces for worship, prayer, and preaching.

The official vision statement of the church in regard to this cohabitation reads: "OCBC is a faith-based community whose vision and mission are nourished by the arts. In our Church life, the arts foster the openness, risk-taking, and imagination manifested in the congregations policies and positions on the seminal social issues of our time."

The remodeling has been a $2.5 million investment, and the ballet company's managing director, Scott Fraser, estimates that there is another million to go. The electrical system has been replaced and the heating and plumbing have been upgraded to current code. They have installed dance floors, sound and lighting equipment, and modern appliances like fire detection and handicapped-access systems. It is now considered a state-of-the-art dance facility. And in exchange for remodeling the building, the dance company gets a twenty-year lease. To ensure that the remodeling investment outlives their long lease, the Ballet Theater insisted that 50 percent of the rent they pay be dedicated, in the terms of the lease, to building maintenance. The congregation happily agreed to this stipulation, as they wanted very much to keep the space current and useful, and felt it would be much easier to include maintenance as a priority, and shield it from the demands of other under-funded good work that they do, by stipulating so in the lease.

The process of remodeling turned up problems that had not been immediately apparent. One surprise came about during the installation of the dance floor in the main sanctuary. In the process, they found that the remnants of the floor they were replacing were not strong enough to support the sprung floor they were installing. So that floor had to be replaced as well. They also discovered, as they repaired the roof, unforeseen water damage that needed attention. Anyone who has repaired an old building will tell you that all this is par for the course.

Scott Fraser believes there are some clear lessons to be learned from the experience.

Old spaces make great venues. In this instance, the sight lines are flexible, with no pillars or posts to interfere. The vaulted ceilings add an air of openness, and the open atmosphere of European architecture enhances the practice of a European art form. An older structure adds weight and gravity to new work by young people.

Arts companies and churches are both altruistic non-profits with brick-and-mortar issues. Whatever the differences in faith issues and belief systems, there is a great deal of common feeling between faith-based organizations and arts companies. Money-making is a secondary issue in the sense that no one goes into either of these areas to make a fortune; financial issues revolve around the capital requirements and human resources for the work that needs to be done. The process of working together was simpler, easier, and more enjoyable than either side first feared would be the case.

Scheduling is not intrinsically a problem. As mentioned earlier, arts venues are primarily concerned with Friday and Saturday nights for performance, and evenings for classes and rehearsals. Churches are primarily concerned with Sunday mornings and usually Wednesday nights, but the rest of the schedule is flexible. Neither organization has any desire to "poach into prime-time" of the other organization.

Arts programming in general creates great opportunities for the "portal experience." This is when someone walks into a church for the very first time, for whatever reason, and becomes aware of an institution and its possibility as a house of worship. The OCBC was averaging 15 to 25 people per Sunday at the start of the partnership, and now averages 40 to 60. In the last ten years there have been eight baptisms; seven have occurred since the ballet company moved in. Pledge income has also risen about 50 percent. Anecdotal evidence points to couples and individuals first discovering the church by attending a dance concert and becoming interested in the church because of the ballet partnership itself. For example, when the ballet company did their Nutcracker concerts in December of 2003, they gave everyone who attended an invitation to return for the OCBC Christmas Eve service. In the past, this service may have drawn 50 people in a good year; but that year, it drew over 200. It blows the dust of stodginess off of the image of the church to involve itself in such partnerships.

In general, the church also finds that arts events make for great outreach projects to the theater community and other non-churched, marginalized groups. Churches have long been associated with exclusive practices in which the congregation is defined by who *can't* come in. Arts events, being open to the public, demonstrate a conscious decision to open the church to anyone who wants to come in; it is a gesture of welcoming and hospitality that echoes the earliest traditions of the church.

Another Partnership Example: The Education Wing

Salem English Lutheran Church in Minneapolis started as an immigrant church that featured services in English, hence the name. In the 1950s they built an education wing with class-rooms, a dining hall, and a playground. But as the congregation evolved and individuals and families moved out to the suburbs and started new churches, Salem found it harder and harder to maintain its underutilized building. Paint was peeling and walls were cracking.

The determined congregation found a match that changed the face of their beleaguered building. The Youth Performance Company (YPC) is a theater program that includes training and performance. It had outgrown its old space. The YPC looked at the education wing for Salem and found a match for their needs. The education wing itself was in good shape, and the urban location was near a number of traffic corridors and was easier to find than the YPC's old location. Further, being located at a church instead of in a warehouse helped soothe the worries of anxious parents about the place they were leaving their kids. Now Salem is free to concentrate on building its congregation instead of saving its building.

6 Theater in the Church, By the Church

POINTS OF ENTRY

As we have seen, many benefits arise from incorporating theater into the life of the Church. These benefits—practical, pas-
toral, theological—comprise an answer to the question, Why
should we bring theater into our church? In this chapter we will
consider the "how" question: How do we go about incorporating theater into the life of our church?

Participation in this work exists on a continuum that ranges
from reading the Bible during worship, to going to see a play
and discussing it, to sponsoring a fully fledged theater program.
Which "point of entry" is best for any given church will depend
on its specific circumstances as indicated by the answers to questions such as: How many people are interested in this possibility? What resources can we put into this effort? What are the
talents and gifts of individuals in our congregation that can
help bring these efforts to fruition? In this chapter we will look
at some of the ways to bring together church and stage that have
a lower impact in terms of the use of physical space, potential
cost, and the numbers of people needed. We will start with the
use of the Bible itself in worship and then go on to other ways

to engage church and community members in faith-related dramatic experience.

Two simple guidelines should be kept in mind no matter what level of complexity is chosen: Don't let inexperience stand in the way, and don't let money or the lack thereof inhibit the process. There are few limits to what can happen when a dedicated group of amateurs undertakes a task. Some of the best work I have ever seen was done in amateur theater, and some of the worst by fully professional companies with high ticket prices. Nor does it require a professional facilitator to guide a discussion of a play or movie. Nonprofessional or inexperienced, we still have the tools to engage in these activities. As for finance, much of what we explore in these pages can be accomplished with little or no money.

Everyone who gets involved achieves a greater acquaintance with the literature of the tradition. And the Church, by using theater, will be able to accomplish things—congregation-building, Christian education, community outreach—upon which it sometimes spends a great deal of money with little outcome.

OPENING UP THE BIBLE:
FROM LECTERN TO BIBLIODRAMA

Just about every church service includes one element that provides a clear connection to theater: the reading of the Bible. The Bible itself is the starting point of church and stage connections that range from the lectern to the youth group and beyond.

The Jewish tradition gives great importance to reading the Bible aloud; moreover, one should read from the Bible itself rather than from a print-out of the text. It was intended to be read that way, and doing less, even in individual study, shortchanges the experience. Reading aloud brings authenticity to our experience of the Bible. It connects us to the roots of the Hebrew Bible, on which we base our faith and which Jesus himself proclaimed out loud (see Luke 4).

Too many people, however, are intimidated by reading the scriptures out loud in a service. I was raised Lutheran in the upper Midwest, and Lutherans especially (as Garrison Keillor has so often pointed out) are brought up to be shy, self-effacing, and inconspicuous. Many Lutherans have trouble reading the text loud enough. Like many others, I needed retraining before I could be heard.

Everyone has experienced a reading in church that was barely audible or read so poorly that it was difficult to follow the meaning at all. Readers, or lectors, need to be reminded: *You are not doing the reading*—it is the text that is speaking, and you are the mouthpiece. You need to be clear, articulate, and loud enough to be heard in the back of the sanctuary.

The first thing a congregation can do to improve this aspect of worship is to practice the reading of the text. I cannot remember how many times I have missed the content of a verse or two because the reader was afraid of making a mistake, so afraid in fact, that we could not hear whether or not a mistake had been made. The best antidote to fear is preparation and familiarity with the material to be read.

I recommend finding an actor in the church and asking him or her to serve as speech coach for readers. The Presbyterians believe there is a place of service for everyone, and it is only natural that someone with some training in the use of the human voice offer up some coaching skills. The actor might say "Enunciate. Breathe deeply. Talk like you want people to understand everything you say. If it is moving material, be moved by it. Speak to the back of the hall, so that everyone can be in on it. The ones in the back are the most shy, and you don't want to deny them the chance of this encounter simply because you are shy too."

If you can't find an actor to volunteer, pay a good one fifty dollars for an occasional hour of coaching. It will be money well spent, just as money paid for candles or flowers to improve the worship space is money well spent. The church's ordained ministers should go through this training as well, and once this type of expertise is installed in the congregation, readers are likely to become adept at coaching one another.

Lectors also improve their delivery of the text by studying it and working to deepen their understanding of its meaning and genre in the context of the Bible. The Psalms, for instance, are a vast collection of poignant song lyrics that can be set to music, adapted, or rewritten for the modern ear. The story of David is one of the first historical biographies. The book of Esther is a novel of assimilation in a different culture and features a strong woman in the leading role.

By studying the Bible we also learn about the nuances of the language within it. We learn that not every sentence in the Bible is to be taken literally, but needs to be viewed in the larger context of what's being said. The phone book is an example of a book to be taken literally. But when Jesus says, "I am the Door," he is not saying he is a literal door, complete with hinges and knob. A fuller understanding of the subtleties of the text informs the lector and improves the ability to proclaim the Word as part of worship.

Adapting biblical texts to be performed is a great educational tool, especially for the young people of the congregation. The goal can be as complex as a full-fledged production or as simple as a two-person dramatic reading designed for a specific church service.

One great point of entry for this is the children's sermon. The children's sermon doesn't have to be a dumbed-down rehash of the regular sermon; it can be an artful presentation of the essence of the reading that elucidates the text for the kids and anyone else in the audience who (like me) needs it presented simply and accessibly.

Another great point of entry is the Christmas service. People expect some sort of presentation of the Christmas story and will not be put off by some creative experimentation that remains faithful to the text. It's also a great opportunity to get the kids up and doing something. Kids love to dress up, they love candles, and parents love to see the little ones participating and maybe even behaving.

Bibliodrama is a type of exercise that works very well in presenting the Bible. In bibliodrama, individuals role-play various characters in the Bible and improvise a way of playing a biblical scene that brings the subject matter closer to the lives of the congregation and the individuals participating. Peter Pitzele used a form of bibliodrama to present rabbinical students with a challenging way of seeing how leaders are tested. "You're Moses; what are your issues?" Pitzele sees the process as "identifying personal challenges embedded in the mythic structures of the Jewish religion, and continually acting them out." For the students, this meant improvising responses to the problems Moses was facing, in much the same way that Moses had to improvise through his circumstances. Role-playing is a standard teaching technique. When creatively applied to engagement with familiar Bible personalities, it blows the dust off tired perceptions of who these people are, and they become much more real to us. In bibliodrama, participants may play the role of actual biblical personalities or create characters whose presence can be inferred from an imaginative reading of the text, such as Simon Peter's mother, who is never present but is named. In bibliodrama the available parts can include inanimate objects such as the Ark of the Covenant or the tomb in which Jesus was buried. Places, animals, and spiritual figures may speak as well. Bibliodrama takes us to an imaginative place in which the entire biblical universe is taken into consideration so that our understanding of the text is more three-dimensional.

The second play in this book's appendix is a chancel drama titled *Herod and Pilate*. This was done as a staged reading (not memorized, no special costumes) on the chancel during a service. It is a Lenten piece and therefore contains little humor. Both pieces exemplify creative use of the scriptures that honors the tradition, speaks to the specific congregation, and invites participation from various members of the congregation, including youth.

Opening up the Bible in these ways has benefits for the entire congregation. Because the Bible was designed to be spoken aloud, we miss something every time we read it silently. By improving our oral presentation of the text we recover some of its authenticity and begin to comprehend how the text has survived for so long. Through practice and study, we increase the consistency with which the text is effectively delivered in the church. More effective presentation of the Bible in church also helps us rediscover the amazing diversity of the biblical literature, allowing congregants to connect to the text in new ways.

MOVIE NIGHT:
BRINGING AUDIENCES INTO THE FRAY

Viewing movies as a group is a low-cost and non-threatening way to use the dramatic arts in the Church's attempt to discuss ideas and engage contemporary culture. The efforts behind putting together movie nights can bear fruit in important ways. Evaluating the stories, characters, meanings, and significance of selected films prepares the ground for more involved use of drama in church, including the actual production of plays. It also helps participants develop the habit of analyzing the content and presentation of such works rather than accepting them uncritically. And if it leads to nothing more than a lively, ongoing movie-discussion group, that is a significant accomplishment in itself.

This is an especially good idea for high school-aged members of the congregation. Going to church to see movies makes church a little less uncool. It is especially important to give kids a chance to form critical thinking skills about what they are looking at. If the films are relatively recent, like new releases on DVDs, they will have even more relevance for this age group.

To organize a movie night, set a schedule, such as the second Friday night of the month, and select movies for the next three months. Make sure the announcement goes out in the church bulletin so parents can be clear about the activity and have an opportunity to ask questions and give input. Plan for a program for one movie each month of the school year.

The selection process can be abetted by assembling some critical materials. Guidebooks like *Leonard Maltin's Family Film Guide* is a good start. There are also several books out that deal with looking at various films as theological texts. Even if such a critique is not available for a film you are considering, you might find it helpful to read one or two to see how professional theologians and critics have made these connections.

Whether you have a teen group, an adult group, or have opened the group to a mixture of ages, film selection is always going to be a sensitive issue. This will apply as much to serious movies with direct religious content as to other films. I could recommend Franco Zefferelli's *Jesus of Nazareth* to the whole family. But *The Last Temptation of Christ* and *Jesus of Montreal* are less suitable for teens who are not yet college-age, despite the fact that they are as good as, or better than, *Jesus of Nazareth* when it comes to teaching about Jesus. Mel Gibson's controversial *The Passion of the Christ* is also problematic for younger teens. Not only is it extremely and graphically violent, it introduces characters and events that are neither biblical nor historical, presents a version of events which, many have commented, promotes anti-Semitic attitudes, and ignores nearly all of Jesus' teaching and ministry. When showing movies about Jesus in church, I feel it is best to go with those that are comprehensive and balanced.

I also recommend that you find one or two films each year that originated as stage plays. Some very good ones that also have religious content include *A Man for All Seasons* and *Becket*. Secular films such as the adaptation of *Death of a Salesman* are also great choices.

In general, you need to look for films that take on serious issues, even in the context of comedy. Choose films that can be readily discussed; stay away from films with obscure symbolism or that are more "heady" and intellectual than you are prepared to discuss. Be sure to include as many members of the group as possible in the selection process; if you pick a film that no one is interested in coming to see, it doesn't matter how good it is. Program your films with great care. Someone has to see the movie first to make sure there aren't surprise sex scenes or garish violence slipped into the show. They've seen it all before, I know, but they don't have to see it in church.

A list of resources that can help in making the selection can be found in appendix B. New books along these lines hit the stores every year.

As participation develops, see if you can find a way to mix and match. Some nights, just teens; others more general. If you have enough people, they could meet in parallel groups that occasionally meet together. Coffee hour could then be a hotbed of modern film criticism.

How to Get Ready: The Facilitator Prepares

Any group such as this needs a facilitator to handle the practicalities of running the group as well as taking the lead in the discussion that follows the viewing of the film. This can be the same person every time, or it can rotate. Co-facilitators can also work; they just need to ensure that, between them, everything that needs to get done gets done

On the practical side, figure out when and where to meet. Be sure you have DVD or video players that work. (When I attended graduate school and took classes with highly credentialed professors, no class that required the use of electronic equipment ever went smoothly. Please rehearse. Know what buttons to push. Plug in the machine, put in the tape or DVD, and make sure it works before anyone gets there.) Make sure someone has rented or purchased a copy of the movie. Be sure to have popcorn and soft drinks available, or ask members to sign up to bring homemade snacks. Especially with teenagers, be careful not to overdo the sugar and caffeine.

The Discussion

As facilitator, you must view the movie in advance and, if possible, read some reviews. If it's an older movie, you might find a study of it or a biography of the writer, director, or star that might shed light or provide background. Seek relevant biblical, theological, and other faith-based resources to help frame the discussion.

Make a list of questions you would like to hear discussed. Be prepared for the conversation to go in directions you did not anticipate. Encourage that. Be sure to make everyone feel welcome to participate, and try to keep the discussion from being dominated by just one or two individuals (including yourself).

THE READERS CIRCLE

Here is an activity that you can do when you have people excited enough to talk about the possibility of doing something with the theater, or even starting a theater company. A theater company does not begin with an office and a desk and a used computer and a box of paper clips. It starts with a mad desire to put up a show. How do people pick which one to do? One way is to get the interested people together in a room, with a script, and read it out loud. Discuss it, and maybe read it again. Then meet the next week and do the same with a different script. You can also do this whole process with no intention of producing a play. You can do it just to learn more about scripts and to serve as the catalyst for discussion of arts and issues.

But if you become motivated to put up a show, keep doing this process until one script jumps out at you—the content, the casting of available actors who seem to fit the roles, timing, everything else—and when most of this falls into place, start getting ready to do a show.

Here are some practical considerations for setting up a readers circle. You can adapt these ideas to your particular situation.

Are you looking to create a monthly discussion group that will read and talk about plays that have a spiritual, moral, or ethical connection? There is a lot to be gained from this, and it will be well worth the effort. Who are the participants? Is it the "fabulous fifties" gang, or the teen group pizza night crowd? Choose your content specifically and carefully. If teens are involved, make sure that parents know about content issues; but at the same time, 14-year-old kids these days know more than 55-year-old doctors did a generation or two ago, so make sure you don't underestimate them. Sex, death, suicide, and family trouble are all part and parcel of their lives, whether directly or indirectly, and if you want them to develop some idea how to survive until they get done with school, church should be a place where honest discussions happen.

If at all possible, try to create a group in which teens and adults can gather together. This is very enriching for both demographic subcultures. Make sure the teens are encouraged to voice their opinions, no matter how goofy they feel or how goofy their ideas are. We need to model for them how a good discussion can happen with people who have different ideas. They see and hear, on television and radio, "discussion" that amounts to nothing more than uncontrolled shouting matches that result in one side feeling they have won and the other feeling as if they have been abused.

If what you want to do is hunt up plays to perform, be selective in the plays you choose. Do not pick shows that require skills, training, and resources that are currently beyond you. You can push yourself, but not over a cliff. And don't do plays that may have huge physical requirements, like lots of lights, massive scenery, or a cast of thousands. Ask everybody involved to bring one play that they have in mind, preferably something they have seen performed and have strong feelings about. As a group, discuss the offerings to eliminate the impossible ones, and then draw straws to find out which play you will read first.

Once you have picked a play, the facilitator has to make sure everyone has a copy. Each person can buy his or her own, just has they would if they joined a club that reads novels picked by *Oprah* or *The Today Show*. Sometimes, however, plays are not as readily available as mainstream fiction and have to be special-ordered from specialty booksellers or publishers such as Dramatists Play Service (www.dramatists.com) or Samuel French (www.samuelfrench.com). Playwrights hope that you will choose this way of doing business rather than making unauthorized photocopies for your group's members. (If you decide to produce the play you will need to pay royalties to compensate the author. More about this later, in the chapter "Let's Put on a Show.")

Pick someone to be the facilitator for each meeting. Ideally, this can be someone who has ambitions as either the director or the producer. Facilitation will help them build the skills needed to take charge of meetings and keep things moving if the discussion gets side-tracked into personal lives or current events. Or you may rotate the job so that everyone gets a chance to gain experience and do the work. The facilitator is responsible for getting the basic labor in place, and should make a checklist to be sure it gets done. The facilitator should also learn how to delegate tasks to members of the group.

The facilitator makes sure that the script is suitable for the age groups participating. He or she should prepare a list of questions to get the discussion going, and may or may not insist on getting through all the questions. Be flexible; if the discussion is great, let it follow its own momentum. If it starts to flag, go to the next question. The facilitator also makes sure that the meeting starts and stops on time; anyone who wants to continue the discussion after the meeting ends can go find a coffee bar and keep going. When meetings like this consistently drag on long past the hour agreed upon, it is common for individuals to choose to stay away.

As for the reading process itself, there are two ways to go about it. The obvious one is to cast people in specific parts, but that can be very limiting. I like the round-robin method. The first person reads the first line, the next person reads the next one, and you just keep going around the table to the end of the play. It doesn't matter who reads which character, because you will all get a chance to do most of them on a random basis. It's good acting practice, and some people will surprise themselves and you with how many different characters they can read well on the spot. It's a great way to get a first pass accomplished on casting if you are going to produce the play; it's the only way to go if you are not.

If some people in the group aren't speaking up loud enough when it is their turn to read, the facilitator needs to stop and remind them to speak up. It's okay to be shy *going to* the theater; it's not okay to be shy *working in* the theater.

The following are some final random guidelines for the facilitator.

Read the script in advance.

Look for and read some reviews from when the play came out. A search on the internet is likely to yield good results for recent plays. If it's an older play, perhaps find a study of it, some commentary or other scholarly works that treat it from a less commercial, more substantial viewpoint. Look for a biography of the writer, director, or star that might shed light. In short, pull together as much background as you can in the time you have to give to this task.

In theater terms, the process of assembling material like this and putting it into a useful form is the job of the *dramaturg* (pronounced with a hard *g*). The work of a dramaturg is called *dramaturgy* (pronounced with a soft *g*). Dramaturgs are very useful when you are studying or producing older, classical plays, and it might be helpful to develop a working relationship with a dramaturg in your area, or to cultivate the skills of an actor who is interested in this aspect of theater.

Find relevant biblical, theological, and other faith-based resources with which to frame the discussion of the moral, ethical, and spiritual issues to be found in the play.

Be prepared for the discussion to go in directions you (the facilitator) did not expect. That's okay. Surprises are a big source of fun and adventure.

The facilitator needs to make arrangements for having water to drink and cups or glasses. Reading aloud is thirsty business.

This is not a time for popcorn.

LET'S GO TO A SHOW

I believe that most people need to see about a dozen shows before they know what theater is about. The shows don't have to be expensive, or professional, or difficult. They can be high school productions, touring shows, experimental plays, script readings, improvisational performances, street theater, fringe theater, or top-buck professional shows. For the first twelve, it doesn't matter. I took a January theater interim when I was in college, and we saw twenty-six plays in twenty-eight days. Thirty years later I am still excited by what I saw.

But don't worry about what kind of show to see. They all count. You just have to get twelve notches on your belt. Then you have achieved a critical mass and will have developed a sense of the great variety available in theater in terms of content, style, performance skill, and so on.

Going to a show with a group of people is a very rewarding activity. Talking about it afterwards is also helpful. Everyone misses something when they are watching a play, and if you have some astute observers who can share what they have seen, you'll have a much better idea of what was going on. And on a good night, you can relive the memorable moments and best punch lines from the production.

Organizing a group of theatergoers from your church adds other dimensions to this activity. It leads to discussions of the plays that might illuminate some aspect of the intersection of faith and life. It demonstrates the deep impact that the arts can have on life and faith, especially when compared to much of the high-profile fare provided by television. It also gives support to groups and individuals who are doing important work in the community. Here are some tips to keep in mind when planning theater outings for interested members of your church.

The age-range of people who make up your group will be an important factor in choosing what plays to attend. You need to make choices that are age appropriate; but be aware that if you have bright teens, from age 14 on up, you can take them to any show you might choose.

Make use of local newspapers, newsletters, and web sites of nearby performance venues to keep track of what's going to be available in your area. During preliminary meetings, ask everyone to bring one suggestion of what to see, along with the reasons they think it would be a good choice. There are many reasons to see a show: a good script, a theater company that you've heard good things about, the fact that someone you know is in the show. Read reviews of the show, if available. In the case of a play that's been around for a long time, such as Arthur Miller's *All My Sons*, read an essay that a critic has written about the play and its content. Narrow down the possibilities until you agree to one show for a specific reason; if the vote is tied, flip a coin. You will need then to determine when to see the show, and assign someone the task of collecting money and buying the tickets (don't forget to look into getting group rates). This is also a good time to choose who will facilitate the after-show discussion.

Plan to have your post-play discussion immediately after the play rather than at a meeting, say, halfway through the next week. The show will be fresh in everyone's mind and you will all enjoy having an after-show drink or dessert. The facilitator needs to be ready with discussion questions; he or she also needs to be responsible for keeping the discussion on track and calling a halt at the appointed hour.

Here are some sample questions for the discussion, adaptable to almost any production:

- Who are the prime characters?
- What is the moral dilemma?
- Why do we care? (If we don't care, then why don't we care?)
- How does this play apply to the life we live today?
- What would Jesus say about this play?

Don't shy away from this last question. I can imagine Jesus commenting, between bites of rice pudding and sips of a nice Australian Shiraz: "I found *All My Sons* to be the perfect illustration of the wages of sin. The father was trying to save the business for his sons, but his cost-cutting decisions killed innocent people, and the ultimate price was the love of the sons he was trying to provide for." Jesus, who seems to me to be very accessible in the New Testament, surely would have been glad to share his opinion on such a great play, so be sure to allow him a part in the conversation.

If you get through all five of those questions, then it's okay to go home.

Sometimes, if you have a large number of people interested in attending plays together, you might want to turn the outing into a fundraiser. With everyone's permission, you arrange for a group rate and then everyone agrees to pay full price. In this way, the event generates a few dollars for a pet project—stage lighting, a food shelf, a new elevator.

Invite people who aren't members of your church or church group. This is a good way to show that church people aren't backward, or anti-intellectual, or afraid of learning, or against artistic expression. This is yet another way to promote the portal experience—getting someone through the doors and introducing them to your church—outside of the context of "going to church." Who knows? If they have a good time, you could invite them to Wednesday night supper or even Sunday services.

Allow me to repeat myself: viewing and reading plays as a group is a low-cost and non-threatening way to use the dramatic arts in the church's attempts to discuss ideas and engage contemporary culture. The efforts behind putting together these nights can bear fruit in important ways. Evaluating the stories, plots, meanings, and significance of selected plays prepares the ground for more involved use of drama in church, such as the actual production of plays. It also helps participants to learn to analyze the content and presentation of such works rather than accept them uncritically. And if it leads to nothing more than a successful, ongoing discussion group, that is a significant accomplishment in itself.

Whatever point of entry you use to bring theater into your church—the lectern, bibliodrama, movie nights, play readings, going to shows—benefits will accrue to all participants, old and young and in between, and the life of the church community will improve accordingly. Here, in summary form, are some of the large benefits you can expect to result from these significant but fun and creative activities:

- The church will no longer be seen as an out-of-touch bastion of the past. It can make vital contributions to our thinking as we make our way in the modern world.
- The shared experience common to all of these activities helps to build community. Community-building is facilitated when people have a reason to be together. Mixed-age group activities open up the possibility for community-building that crosses and transcends the demographic lines we often apply to our organizations.
- Participants develop critical capacities as they engage in the creative process and analyze the creative work of others.
- Participants develop the ability to apply biblical and church teaching to contemporary situations and the arts. The wisdom of the Bible is current and relevant. Participants will find themselves applying faith-based wisdom to more and more situations because of the habits developed during these activities.
- Kids and parents who participate together invest valuable time in their family relationships.

7

Let's Put on a Show

Let's say you have some motivated people in your congregation who want to take this whole thing to the next level and start producing theater for your church. Let's assume that you have gone through the experience of doing some chancel drama and that you've talked about what makes good spiritually oriented theater. Perhaps some of the participants have experience in theater, professional or amateur. Let's also assume that you have a space in which to perform and to rehearse. You start to produce your own theater when you become so excited about doing a specific play or program that you *just have to do it*.

Keep this in mind: no one can tell before hand whether the show will be a wonderful experience or a screaming nightmare, whether it will be loved and adored by a grateful public or greeted with anger, spite, and empty seats. Most shows fall somewhere in between. Keep your expectations in line with reality; make sure you are doing it for more than just self-education or box-office receipts. Some of the best shows I have been a part of were not commercial successes, and some of the commercial successes were not artistically valuable. There is a mixed bag of rewards awaiting you, so don't be choosy about which ones you end up with. Be grateful for the chance to do something inspiring, even if you and the cast are the only ones inspired by it.

START SLOWLY

I recommend beginning with something simple. When I worked at Grace-Trinity Church in Minneapolis, I had three teenaged guys under my supervision: Mike, Jacob, and Ruben. I suggested that they take two parables and rewrite them in modern-day circumstances. They exceeded my instructions and cleverly combined two parables. This grew into a presentation called "The Prodigal Son and His Brother and Not Only That, but the Unwise Groomsmen," which Mike, Jacob, Ruben, and some additional recruits performed during the church's Shrove Tuesday pancake dinner.

In their retelling, the story began with a man in North Carolina. He had two sons and a nice, family-oriented restaurant that they all operated together. One son wanted to go to New York and open his own, trendy, restaurant. He asked his father for his inheritance and went to New York, where he blew all his money on a riotous Big Apple lifestyle, all the while telling himself he was going to open this great restaurant. When the money ran out, he was so poor that he had to take a job at a wedding reception hall in New Jersey and had to content himself with eating the leftovers from the plates he was clearing. He thought, "If I was back with my dad, he'd at least give me a job with three square meals a day."

One night he was working a wedding that had three groomsmen (we didn't have enough girls to act as bridesmaids). Two of the groomsmen had brought umbrellas and one had not. While they were standing around waiting for the groom, it began to rain. The groomsman who got wet had to go home to change, and by the time he came back everyone was inside and the bouncer wouldn't let him in because he was no longer wearing a tux. The Prodigal Son witnessed the scene and had a revelation: "When your time is up, it's up! If you aren't ready, it's too late! I want to go back home to my pop and apologize before he dies. I'm so ashamed I don't want to go, but I've—I've got to!"

The end follows the story from Luke. The father and son are reconciled, and then, at the urging of the father, the brothers are reconciled. But the language of the scene is modernized to bring home the idea that these old stories are about us, today.

The process through which this presentation came about illustrates the many ways that theater can improve a congregation's spiritual experience *and* be done simply and inexpensively. It had educational implications for the participants: We reviewed the parables we knew. We talked about which ones would be good to perform at a pancake supper. Ruben's inspiration to combine two parables shed new light on each one. As actors, the guys had great energy; they hammed it up, made it funny, and had a good time. They made the material their own. By virtue of their participation they now have a working knowledge of the breadth of topics covered in the parables and a sense of the storytelling tradition of which parables are a part. The performance was very well received and the audience benefited from the insights of the performance team.

"The Prodigal Son and His Brother and Not Only That, but the Unwise Groomsmen" was a modest start but it is the sort of activity that opens the door to greater use of all that theater can offer a congregation.

We have seen that combining church and stage can be simple or complex, depending upon the level of involvement to which a congregation can commit. The following are some basic guidelines for heading in the direction of full-scale play production.

CHOOSING A PLAY

If your congregation is taking the step toward full-scale play production, the first challenge is to choose a play. Chances are that one or more of the individuals who are taking leadership in this endeavor have certain plays in mind—plays they have seen or read or appeared in somewhere else that have touched them deeply and that they feel would benefit others if only they could see them.

Such plays may have specifically religious content or may come from secular sources. What they will most likely have in common is a tendency to deal with important issues and show people in the process of working through moral conflicts. Whatever its source—a Greek playwright 2,500 years ago, Arthur Miller in the 1950s, or a local playwright struggling to find a stage for her or his newest work—a good play will have something to say to the community.

Choosing a play requires an evaluation process. Part of that process is being aware of who is available to do the acting; you don't want to fall into the trap of choosing a play for which you will have no suitable actors. This subject is dealt with in greater detail below. I recommend that the core group of participants get copies of plays they are interested in doing and read them aloud. As with hearing the Bible proclaimed in church, it is important to hear a play out loud. Divide the parts up among those present, listen to the words, and discuss the experience afterwards.

It is wise to begin with a play that is specifically connected to the church. *Becket* by Jean Anouilh is at the top of my list, with its tough, realistic language, its historicity, and its story of a man of God grappling with his conscience in a world of power and politics. In a similar vein are other classics such as John Osborne's *Luther* and Robert Bolt's *A Man for All Seasons.*

It is important to point out again that plays are, more often than not, copyrighted works of art. This means that the owner of the copyright—in most cases the playwright or translator—must be compensated for his or her work. You must follow instructions found on the copyright page of the published play, contact the person or organization administering the copyright, establish that your organization is eligible to produce it, and pay the appropriate royalty fees. (An actual royalty notice is included on the copyright page of this book in reference to the plays found in appendix A.) Royalties are frequently determined according to the amateur or professional status of the producing organization, the number of performances, the number of seats in the house, the ticket price, and other such factors. Your church will pay much less to put on *All My Sons* than will a professional theater company or a university theater department. Producing a play without paying the royalty is like stealing a book from the publisher's warehouse—the author will not be compensated. Because producing a play is a public endeavor with legal and ethical ramifications, it is imperative to follow the rules for the sake of your conscience, your organization, and the continuing flow of arts and ideas in society.

Exceptions to the rule include plays in the public domain such as those of Shakespeare. Older works such as plays by Molière, Chekhov, and the ancient Greeks, that have been translated into English may or may not be in the public domain depending upon the age of the translation. Always check the text of the published version's copyright page for details. You will also find collections of plays, typically short plays for children or educational use, that are royalty-free. Again, always check the copyright page and follow the instructions given there.

THE PRINCIPLE LEADERS OF THE EFFORT

Don't let inexperience prevent you from doing a show. No one knows how to do something until they do it. Make use of the materials at hand, including the people. Everyone begins with little experience and grows from there. If you have the luxury of having some people with theatrical experience, great. No matter where you are starting, these thumbnail sketches of the key leaders will give you an idea of what each role requires and the type of person who might best fill it.

Producer

In commercial theater the producer primarily puts together the cash to pay for the mounting of a show and oversees how that money is spent. In a non-commercial situation the producer's role is typically more varied than that, and he or she is often challenged to accomplish more with less. The producer is in charge of the big picture, such as the budget, getting a license to produce the play (if it is a copyrighted work), and making sure that the royalties get paid. He or she needs also to be concerned with the small details, such as getting an aqua-foam washcloth for scene six. When all is delegated—the making of costumes and scenery and so on—the producer is the person who does what needs to be done that isn't getting done. She is the firefighter, the troubleshooter, the one who rolls up her sleeves and says "I'll do it." The producer should be the type of person who is not afraid of getting her hands dirty and who does not complain about it, either. When the buck stops, it stops with the producer.

Director

The director needs to be thoroughly familiar with the show and have a strong vision of how it will play out. In the old days, actors directed each other, and most directors have some acting experience. If you don't have anyone with directing experience, choose a good actor to direct. The director does not have all the answers, but knows how to make decisions and keep things moving. She or he is like a factory foreman who has to put each piece together first and then make all the pieces work as a unit. This person should be able to operate with an iron fist in a velvet glove; to get things done and keep things moving without being antagonistic. The director provides direction. It doesn't matter if the director sometimes gets lost; it *does* matter if the director gets stuck. Keep moving.

Technical Director

The Technical Director (TD) is the kind of person who can read the directions for hooking up a computer or stereo and make it work on the first try. Most technical equipment is made so that amateurs can run it, but tech work is not to everyone's taste. Many theater people have done some of it in high school or college, and they know whether they like it or not. I worked tech for a while and I enjoyed being responsible for the deeper dimension that running the lights and music can bring to a show. TDs are like television's MacGyver, who was notorious for using unusual but *available* props that uickly got the work done. Problems are solved with creative finesse, and duct tape is often involved.

The TD also needs to be dedicated to safety. When I produced the Minnesota Fringe Festival, I required the TD of each show to be in charge of safety issues such as making sure the fire exits aren't blocked and ensuring that the electricity is wired safely. He or she must be the "safety conscience" of the production. My TDs were authorized to shut down any show and any performance if people were not safe. I was once injured on an unsafe set, and I know others injured on unsafe sets; I consider safety to be of utmost importance. Make sure everyone knows that safety issues are brought to the TD. The TD is also authorized to challenge the director on safety issues (ideally, this is done away from the cast, unless danger is imminent). The director should always say "thank you" when safety issues are raised. No show is worth risking anyone's life or limb.

The TD is in charge of running a technical rehearsal prior to the final dress rehearsal. This will be described in greater detail below.

Stage Manager

The stage manager (SM) is traffic cop, time keeper, holder of actors' valuables, the director's right hand, mediator, finder of lost props, and generally the one who holds everything together during the performance. The role of the SM is, in other words, critical.

The SM must be ultra-organized, responsible, and trustworthy. During rehearsals, the SM follows the script, noting the director's blocking and helping forgetful actors with dropped lines. During the show's run, the SM makes sure props are where they belong, keeps track of actors so they don't miss entrances, and cues any light, sound, or set changes.

It is the perfect role for individuals who want to be immersed the dramatic action but are not inclined to perform onstage.

House Manager

The house manager is the face of the theater to anyone who comes to see the show. Hospitality is a Christian virtue, and this person is the hospitable one who solves every problem for the audience. This should be someone who likes people, or can at least pretend to. Anyone who has waited on tables or worked retail can do this, but again it needs to be someone who will project a cheery disposition no matter what is going on.

The house manager will need to assemble a crew to help with various tasks. If you have a place that seats more than fifty people, try to have at least two people to sell tickets and then an usher or two. This is a great way to bring someone into the process who isn't really ready for a larger commitment, give them a little experience, and make them susceptible to catching the theater bug.

Have two people count the money, both before and after the show. Account for everything, including shortages and overages. In twenty years of independent theater, I have never had a customer bounce a check. It's a nice audience to deal with, with only very rare exceptions.

The house manager and her helpers are in charge of seating. They arrange the chairs neatly before anyone gets there, make sure the place is clean and presentable, and ensure that no chairs are broken or dirty. (Stagger the chairs so that audience members are not staring at the back of someone's head.) Then they count the chairs. This is to prevent them from selling too many tickets *and* to make sure that they don't stop selling tickets before the show is sold out. If a show is selling out, ushers need to know where the unclaimed seats are, and they need to report to the house manager. It's okay to ask people if a chair is saved or not.

"Polite but firm" is the mantra for anyone in these customer contact and staffing positions. *Polite* means treating people with respect, and that includes actors, audience members, and all the staff. *Firm* means that when a problem arises, you resolve it. You do not leave it unresolved.

CASTING A PLAY

Almost every play that gets produced comes from a list of maybe ten plays that a producer or group wants to do. They sift through the possibilities and make a choice according to the availability of actors to perform the roles in the show. The great Broadway hits in the days before television often started with the actors who were available, and then the show was written around them. Who is available is very important. Start with that.

At the same time, don't put people in way over their heads. It's okay to challenge people, but in this environment, which is a sort of community theater, don't take on highly complicated shows or shows with tough acting assignments unless you have adequate depth in talent.

A very small production can be done with no auditions. You just walk around and draft people who would be good at particular roles, and when you have talked enough reliable people into committing, you are ready to begin.

If you are holding auditions, though, provide ample time. Running auditions is an involved process. First, you need to set up a pair of rooms so that people who are waiting their turn cannot hear or see the person who is currently auditioning. It is a very vulnerable process for everyone, so reduce their exposure. Have your stage manager there to meet people and coordinate bringing them in and out, answering questions, and so on.

Second, have people assigned to specific times, and keep to the schedule. Fifteen to twenty minutes is good for each actor; five minutes for them to do a monologue they have prepared, five minutes for you to have them read a couple of parts that you envision them doing, and five minutes for questions or redoing something. Then take a few minutes to make notes. At the end, say, "Thank you very much for auditioning. We'll call you." Treat them with respect. If they can't be in the show, you still want them to buy a ticket or work on the show in some other way.

If someone goes over the time allowed that you have given them for their prepared monologue, remember that this is a bad sign, that they are treating you with a lack of respect, and that this is the beginning of more problems. After they have gone one minute over, stop them and say, "Excuse me, but we asked for a five minute monologue, and you are at six minutes now. We need to keep moving." If they respond gracefully and cooperatively, you have someone who can take direction. If they argue with you, you have someone who is going to try to be the second director. You never want two directors. Steer clear of this type of person even if their acting is the best you see in the auditions.

Keep in mind that throughout the audition you may be very excited about a particular person, but then the next person comes in who is *so much better!* Or one person seems to be a good choice for any of three roles, and two other people can do only one role out of the three. Remember that you are in the middle of a *process:* Make no decision before its time. Start the deciding process *after* you have seen everyone, and don't say anything to anybody at all, ever, until you have decided about all the roles.

Then make the calls. For those who have been cast, say something like "Thank you for auditioning. I'd like to offer you the part of Eddy. The first rehearsal is on Tuesday at 6:00 p.m. Please call me to confirm your acceptance. I am looking forward to working with you." After the roles have been cast and the actors have accepted their parts, contact those who did not make the cut: "Thanks for auditioning. We can't offer you anything this time around, but we appreciate your time and effort, and would like to thank you with two free tickets to opening night." That's if you really did like them. If you think they should never audition again, especially if they are members of the church, say, "We can't offer you a role this time around, but are hoping you could find a way to help us out backstage or in the box office or ushering. If so, that would be great. Call me and let me know if you are available." Whatever the decision, treat everyone with respect and let them know that their efforts and abilities can be an asset to the production offstage as well. Remember, those who have auditioned have put themselves on display for you. Do not wholly reject anyone. Everyone can contribute in some way to a successful production.

A PRODUCTION TIMELINE

Most church theater programs do only one show a year. If you do two, you are ambitious; if you do three, you have a theater company. If this is your first one, I suggest a long timeline. Here is a sample timeline to use as a model.

September: Announce that you are doing a show in the spring. Assemble your team of principal leaders and distribute copies of the script.

October: Start talking to people that you want to consider for acting roles in the show. It is acceptable to offer key roles to actors, especially those with some experience, prior to the official auditions.

First half of November: Hold auditions for parts that have not been cast.

Early December: Announce the casting decisions. Distribute copies of the script to cast members.

January: Start rehearsals.
Mid-March: First full run-through.
Early April: Technical rehearsal and full dress rehearsal(s).
Mid-April: Opening night.

Once rehearsals commence, plan on having a brief (no more than an hour) production meeting every two weeks with house management, technical director, stage manager, producer, director, and anyone else involved in a critical technical role so that everyone knows what everyone else is doing. This way nothing falls through the cracks and there are no surprises when technical and dress rehearsals begin.

With this timeline, the technical and house management people will have plenty of time to prepare—and preparation is 90 percent of their jobs. Get another group—perhaps led by the house manager—to begin the marketing process, especially calling people who might be interested in coming to the show. Have them keep track of what the actors are doing in this respect as well. Actors are a great resource for helping to fill the seats, but they need to be done with all of their marketing work at least ten days before opening night. They need to forget about selling tickets, assume there will be an audience, and focus on the performance.

RUNNING A REHEARSAL

The director needs to be as organized as possible, making full use of the stage manager to keep on task. There is nothing worse than a director who is winging it and gets mad at the actors because he isn't ready with the next thing to do. The director must always be ahead of the actors and the process.

In the case of a shorter play, do two read-throughs at your first rehearsal. Don't talk much about the play before the first read. Do some talking after the first read-through, and do some more after the second read. Don't let people stop the reading with questions; you are trying to get the whole show into their heads. Having a strong sense of the whole will help them with their own parts. If you are doing a longer play, settle for one initial read-through followed by a good, substantive discussion.

Also, and this is important: Lay down the law at the first meeting, before anyone says anything, that actors are not to give *notes* (meaning "ideas" or "advice") to any other actors. All those ideas go to the director, who will decide what ideas to implement. In other words if the actor playing Stanley has a suggestion for the actor playing Stella, he needs to communicate that to the director, in private, and not to Stella. Decisions are the job of the director, not the actor. Respect the chain of command. Doing a show is not a democracy. It is a benevolent dictatorship. The director has the best interests of the entire cast and the whole show in mind, and must not be thwarted by actors (well-intentioned or not) in the process. Actors and directors are advised to have such discussion "off line," as it were, and to conduct them with tact and respect.

For rehearsal purposes it is important to break the show down into workable sections. What are the hard parts of the play? Who are the actors that need the most work? What segments are clearly divisible into bite-sized chunks? The answers to these questions will vary from show to show. Go easy at first, and assign for practice enough material but not too much. Don't require anyone to memorize their roles until you have all had a good chance to understand what the play is about, what the scenes are about, what each line is about. If actors start memorizing too early, it may instill bad habits that become impossible to break. Remind them that a play is a living, breathing organism of many parts, and they won't know how it all comes together until the curtain goes up opening night. In the early stages, they need to be open to changes, suggestions, and ideas. They need to be open to taking direction.

Try to have everyone make at least one rehearsal a week, with the principal characters rehearsing twice, depending on the play.

Every show that uses even a small number of technical requirements (lighting changes, dress changes, set changes, music and sound cues, etc.) needs to have a technical rehearsal prior to the final dress rehearsal. At this rehearsal the technical director is the king or queen. The actors *must* participate, but they need to understand that they are not there to have fun or refine their performances. They are there to run through, sometimes several times, each and every moment of the show in which the technical staff need to respond to tech cues. If they make a mistake, or something doesn't work, the technical director will make them do it again and again until it is done correctly, and the actors must participate and cooperate in full. This is a small but necessary price for having a good technical show. Everyone needs to chip in and maintain a good attitude.

The final step is to have one or more dress rehearsals. Theoretically, a dress rehearsal runs through the entire show, with full costumes and technical effects, with no stopping other than any scheduled intermission. Theatrical superstition holds that a bad dress rehearsal leads to a great opening night. But rather than depending on the superstition coming true, I suggest that everyone make every effort to accomplish a strong dress rehearsal so that every participant goes into opening night with a strong positive attitude and boundless enthusiasm.

MARKETING THEATER WITH A ZERO-BASED BUDGET

This part of the chapter has nothing to do with the content of your show. This is about how to get people to come and see what you have done. You want to promote beyond your congregation, lest they begin to feel as if they are being herded into the pens every few weeks to see a show. You want to go out to the community at large so that the community will come in to you.

For some people, *marketing* is a very scary word. What it really means, though, in the context of theater, is this: *Identifying your audience, getting in touch with them, and making a compelling case for them to buy a ticket to your show.* That's not so scary. Everything you do in marketing is about making that decision as easy as possible for the buyer. If you flatten all the resistance in front of the customer, they will roll gently to your door. All you need to do is the work.

Two main rules predominate in the marketing of church and stage: Don't spend money until you absolutely have to; and use common sense in a disciplined manner.

Remember that you are competing for attention with everything out there—every movie, every TV show, every web site, every band. So work the percentages. Do whatever you can to improve your odds. The advice that follows is meant to be something of a checklist. Through continued use, you may add modifications that make sense for your group. It should be modified, updated, and systematized into an operating manual for marketing your specifictheatrical product to your potential audiences.

Marketing is essentially the job of the producer. If he or she doesn't do it directly, the producer still needs to make sure it gets done by assigning responsibility for the various tasks and providing the necessary tools.

Remember, a show without an audience is just a rehearsal.

Let's start by looking at a timeline for marketing your show. Then we'll go back and look at the specific tasks that need to be done and how to go about them with a crew of volunteers.

Marketing Timeline

The marketing timeline is not merely a list of ideas to think about. It is a necessary and practical tool. Each show you do will benefit from having a physical timeline, with key dates and events and places to write in new information and actions taken, hanging on the wall of Church & Stage Central, whether that be a corner of your pastor's office, an alcove in the all-purpose room, or a table in the boiler room.

Ninety days before opening night

1. Start your mailing list: Begin collecting names, addresses, phone numbers, and e-mail addresses of people in your primary audience and beyond. This should be an ongoing process that everyone involved in the production contributes to. It should therefore be systematized and automatic. Make a point of collecting new mailing list information at every meeting. Collate the lists and weed out duplicates.

2. Get a list of the neighborhood or local newspapers for each member of your cast. Call each newspaper and find out how to submit information: Do they prefer electronic images? What are their deadlines? Will they accept information submitted by e-mail? What kind of stories are they looking for? Suggest they write a feature about your show, but be prepared to settle for a captioned photo. Write their key dates on the timeline for the show.

3. Check into the "specialty" newspapers in the area—the ones that cover certain communities, religious, ethnic, or geographic. For example, make sure African American participants get coverage in any local black publications, so that members of the African American community know they are welcome in the audience.

4. Take advantage of any opportunity for promotional showcases. Perform excerpts from the show, or do readings, at coffeehouses, bookstores, open stages, and anywhere else you can think of.

5. Begin compiling a press kit to be sent to any and all media. The local press is inundated with kits from shows, so in order to stand out from the crowd, keep it extremely short and sassy. It is imperative to include an intriguing page with all the relevant info: what, who, where, and when; two press clips from previous performances if you have them, and a great photo from a past show or of members of the current cast working together on the new show.

6. Line up sponsors for your postcards and programs. In exchange

for paying your printing/mailing costs, your sponsor's logo can be run (very prominently) on the card. You can also recoup some of your costs by selling ads to run in your production's program. Charge, for example, $75 for a full page, $45 for a half page, $25 for a quarter page. Local merchants are often very open to spending a small amount of money so that a few hundred audience members might see their ad and develop an impression of the business as one that cares about community.

Sixty days before opening night
Mail your press kits. Keep a few extra copies, just in case local media requests them at the box office during the festival.

Thirty days before opening night
1. Send postcards—with good, clear images and graphics—to all the individuals on your mailing list. Be sure to include all of the important info: location, times, dates, and phone number. Everyone involved in the production should carry postcards with them at all times, so they can give them to interested friends they run into in the course of normal daily activities. More tickets are sold in the grocery store than you might realize.
2. Call the local media and give them the scoop. Don't expect your phone message to be returned, but leaving a voicemail reminder can't hurt. Give them all the essential information and make sure they can reach you if they'd like to call back.

Two weeks before opening night
Get on the phone! Call your friends and neighbors to remind them to mark their calendars for opening night. Try setting up a phone-a-thon so that the whole list gets worked through. Calls should take about thirty seconds apiece, especially when you are merely leaving a message. This may not be anyone's idea of fun, but it is also not a root canal. Have a phone night where you

bring in pizza and Diet Coke and buzz through the list; compare notes for what people said and how many reservations you have.

One week before opening night
Encourage everyone to e-mail their friends and family, one more time, about opening night. Keep daily track of how many reservations you have, and figure out if you have enough. This is technically called "demand forecasting." It helps you ascertain how many chairs to set up, or whether you need to add shows or go back and the phones and start calling more people. If you don't have enough, go back to the phone lists, call the board and staff of the church, and tell them that you want a big opening night and you don't have enough reservations. Be honest, be clear, and sound slightly desperate without begging. That's my advice, anyway.

Night of show
Make sure everything is clean and ready early. Make sure that transactions can happen quickly. Two people taking money is best. At least two ushers are a good idea, especially to help anyone who needs assistance. Make sure the bathrooms are clean and smelling fresh. Have a sign up that says Make Checks Payable To: Whatever Church so people can be ready when they get up there.

The Many Tasks of Marketing

The timeline gives you the big picture, and you will need to change it, massage it, and sometimes perhaps turn it nearly upside down depending on all the variables such as number of participants to help with the work, actual money in hand to spend on tasks, number of media outlets to contact, and on and on. But now let's look at some of the specific ideas and tasks that must be dealt with in the context of the marketing timeline.

Identifying your primary audience

Your *primary audience* consists of the people you know, the people your cast and crew know, your friends, relatives, coworkers, fellow congregants, and neighbors. These people are the ones most likely to make up your opening night audience. They are the ones who will see the show and talk about it. In the case of a church, we are talking about:

- families, friends, neighbors, and business associates of the actors and all other show participants
- congregants and staff, their families, friends, and business associates
- industry people, i.e., people from neighboring churches, or churches in the denomination, or nearby schools that have theater departments, history departments, etc.
- people from other local theater organizations
- any person who has entered your church building and for whom you have contact information (these are really good names to get; anyone who has "passed through the portal" knows where the church is, what it does, and where to park)

Build your primary audience list by having everyone who is involved in the production collect the names, addresses, phone numbers, and e-mail addresses of everyone they know who fits the criteria of being a member of the primary audience. Share a method for recording the names; you might want to use 3 x 5 cards, one for each contact. At one or more points in the process, gather all the cards together and merge them, at the same time purging duplicate listings. This master list should be entered into a computer; each name should be accompanied by the name of the participant who contributed it. A computer-savvy member of your crew can set up the list in such a way that it can be sorted in a variety of ways; for example, you might sort it by zip code or neighborhood or according to the name of the person who put the name on the list.

Making contact

Take a moment to visualize an audience of one hundred people. It took work to get each one of them into his or her seat.
For contacting the primary audience I advocate a system I call
"PEPC" (pronounced the same as the soft drink, one of several
caffeinated staples among theater folks; I myself am dedicated
to Diet Coke), which stands for "Postcards E-mail Phone Calls."
One hundred people in the audience may represent 200 phone
calls, 400 postcards and 500 e-mails. *You must wrestle each ticket
buyer to the ground* (figuratively speaking), one at a time. Some
people will show up anyway, but *you and the cast and crew must
take personal responsibility* for having an audience. And I have to
say, it is a good thing artistically for the performers and staff to
be thinking about the audience. It makes everyone more grateful for the people who do attend, and it encourages a sense of
hospitality toward those brave souls daring to risk their time and
money to witness our adventure.

To get the PEPC process rolling, print the full audience list
and divide it among the participants—the entire cast and crew.
Each participant will be responsible for contacting the people
whose names they contributed to the list; however, be reasonable and try to divide the work evenly, and don't be afraid to
contact a stranger.

When using postcards, be sure that all the pertinent information is included and prominently displayed: title, address,
phone number and e-mail address, price, directions, and where
to park. Make sure that the recipient can get in touch and make
a reservation—by phone, fax, or e-mail. If your church has a web
site and you are using it to promote the show (and if you are
not, shame on you!) include the web address, too.

The same goes for making contact via e-mail. E-mails, un-
like postcards, can be easily personalized. You can paste in the
basic text, and then add a special note to a particular friend:
"Remember when we ran the lights for *Promises, Promises* back
in junior year? This time I'll be standing IN the spotlight—you

oughta come out and see the show!" Don't be afraid to let your enthusiasm show.

For making phone calls, write out a little speech giving the pertinent information about the show, and be prepared for the probability that you will be leaving a lot of voicemail messages: "Hi, this is Eddy Gordetsky from Lake Avenue Church. We are doing a production of *Becket*, the play about the quarrel between the Archbishop of Canterbury and the King. It's really great! It opens on January thirteenth and we'd love it if you could be there opening night. We're trying to sell out the show. Please call us at 333-4444 with a reservation or if you have questions. Tickets are only fifteen dollars."

Additional information might also be helpful: "We've got plenty of free parking right in our own lot" or "The 74 and 16 buses stop just half a block away and run till midnight." Make people feel that you would welcome their return call for further information. This is essential to developing the comfort level people need to proceed with the decision to purchase a ticket and attend the show.

I can't emphasize it enough: Make the calls. Send the e-mails. Ten days before opening night, call everyone on your mailing list who has not responded with a ticket reservation or a firm "no" (this call will ideally be made by the person who put them on the list in the first place) for one last pitch.

Everyone involved needs to make these phone calls, and no excuses are acceptable. *If you make the calls, you will be okay.*

If you don't make the calls and send the e-mails, *nothing else will save you.* Not rave reviews, not a great show, not a great photo, not advertising. Nothing.

Group sales

Group sales possibilities should be handled by a group sales coordinator, as these sales usually require extra attention to logistics. This person can be doing other things for the production, but the point is to make sure that one person knows that she or he is responsible for this effort. Group sales efforts should be tracked on a show-by show basis so that you can accumulate knowledge about this market as your theater program develops. Groups from other churches seem to be a natural fit, but those groups often take a long time to make decisions, so do not be surprised if it takes a year or even two before your neighborhood churches start coming over in larger numbers to see your work. It is possible, too, that they will see it as a distraction to their own programming, in which case the alliance might not be as natural as you would expect.

A special note to the group sales coordinator: In my experience, Christian groups seeking outings such as theater productions are notorious for bad manners. Do not be surprised if they act as if God has chosen them to receive a special deal at the expense of your church and theater program. Every salesperson knows that they cannot give away the store, and must be ready to deal with such customers, whatever type of group they represent, politely and firmly. It is not out of line to remind a rude customer to mind his or her manners.

Pricing

Never charge less than the price of a movie ticket. We're human beings, this is live performance, and it's hard work. It's worth more. A reasonable price in 2005 is $10, or $15 for a show that has some experienced actors or costuming or lights or scenery. If you are giving away some of the proceeds, $20 is a good price. In such cases, use the fundraising aspect to increase the incentive to buy tickets; make sure you tell everyone that you are giving, say, 10 percent of the proceeds to the cause (and make sure that the first check you write after expenses is that 10 percent check). Leave a collection basket at the door so that people can make an extra contribution to the cause or to the theater program. Those little baskets can hold some big surprises.

Press relations

Here is an important rule about working with the press: *All marketing is about temptation. Lead them into it.* In other words, do not oversell. Do not go on and on. Write a press release that is interesting, catches their attention, and makes them interested in knowing more. Leave them wanting to know more. You will be asking people to risk their time and their money on your show, and that means making your case quickly and compellingly. Stress opening night in the press release, and include the phone number and web site address for more information.

You can't tell anyone, the press included, everything about your show. That's what the show itself is for. Tell them just enough so that they want to inquire further.

All your promotional material, whenever possible, should contain a listing of your cast and crew members, because the number one reason people attend an opening night is that they know someone in the show. Don't worry about personnel changes that may or may not happen as work on the production continues. It's more important to have things out on time than it is to have them perfect.

Make sure to involve your neighborhood newspapers. *This is the single most overlooked opportunity for coverage in the business.* Get every single member of your cast, and especially the church itself, to find their neighborhood paper—especially the people in the promo photo—and sent out releases saying, "Neighborhood resident Jane Petty is appearing in the Westminster Church Production of Becket. . . ."

Call the small radio stations, and the big ones. Tell them you have someone who is willing to talk on the subject. Offer them tickets to give away on the air. College radio and small timers have small audiences, but they are the peer group leaders and opinion shapers for the public at large. Work on having sound bites, thirty-second snippets that quickly cover the important points and do so succinctly.

When working with the press, another rule says: *Make your deadlines.* After the deadline, your news is dead. Keep in mind that neighborhood papers are usually monthly, so for the July issue you may need to submit your press materials by mid-May.

Call each and every paper you expect to approach, well in advance, and ask about their deadline. Also, offer them complimentary tickets (comps) to a performance. Getting them in to see the show can be a real boon to growing the audience base. Press people like comps because their work is usually underpaid, and free is free. By focusing your efforts on a sold-out opening night, you pack the house, create word-of-mouth early, and get the news out to your new audience while helping sell tickets down the line. This will all add up to a future in which such papers will look to you for news and maybe even preview your show.

Promotional photos

Here is another important rule about dealing with the press: *a good photo or image is your best marketing investment.* All you really need these days is a good point-and-shoot digital camera, someone who knows how to use it well, and the means by which you can ship your photo electronically. Take several photos and choose the best to show the press. Make sure you don't shoot it from too far away—many publications will run a very small copy of your photo, and faces work best. Show two characters, in costume, reflecting whatever the conflict is in the show, but focus from the shoulders up to achieve the greatest clarity.

A good promo photo will get attention for your press release, whether newspapers run the photo or not. If they print your photo, people will more likely read the information about your show. If they use the photo, it's like getting a free ad every time it runs, so it's worth your time and a little investment to make sure you have a good image.

When you print up your pictures, *pick just one.* Use that one on your postcard, your poster, the program, write a caption for it, and to send out to the press. Send photos to any publication that has any interest at all in what you are doing. Papers that run theater reviews are first, of course, but don't limit your thinking to theater and art. Look for publications within your denomination—newspapers, newsletters, and the like. If your show or your cast or your play is Irish, for example, or African American, or about colleges, make sure to send your promo to the Irish or African American or college papers. The same goes for radio shows. They are more interested in your show if they see a picture, and more likely to let you on the air if they like the picture.

Also, make sure that the box office has photos available for the press. Three copies should cover you on opening night, and at least one every other night. Letting the local newspaper's reviewer exit the theater with a photo makes it possible that his review will run with a photo, making it all the more prominent on the page. That's good news for you—if the show has more performances scheduled after the paper comes out, you may sell more tickets. But even without more performances, it's good news because it is exposure for your church and for the theater program you are running within it.

Promotional posters

Posters should be displayed only where they are welcome. If you put one on every lamppost in town, it's called *sniping*. Sniping is illegal in Minneapolis, where I live and work, and they enforce it. It makes the neighborhood look trashy, it's largely ineffective, and it's usually done by people who don't want to make the phone calls.

If you want to put up posters, make sure to ask permission. Put them up in coffee houses, church bulletin boards, or other public places that allow them and that are frequented by pedestrians (it's hard to read a poster while driving by in a car). Make a list of all the places that are poster-friendly and develop an efficient way of making the rounds the next time you do a show. Make sure that all of the standard promotional information is prominently displayed on every poster.

Ticket deals

With every show, no matter where or when, you will always find people who are looking for a deal or a free ticket. I've got some rules about the *when, how much,* and *who* of giving away seats to a show.

Provide complimentary tickets to whomever you want on opening night. Find groups who are poor by definition, like people in halfway houses or homeless shelters or senior citizen centers, and give them twenty or so tickets to make sure you have a crowd to play to. If people can't get in for the first night because of that, it creates more of a buzz. You can usually add shows if demand increases. You can never cut back on a show because there is a small house.

If people need a break and can't come opening night, you can sell them two for the price of one for any show except closing night.

Give no comps or two-for-ones on closing night. They will ask. Tell them No.

Comps should go to people who helped you put up the show, people who are broke, people who don't have an income, people who gave birth to members of the cast and crew, members of the press and other media, or other indispensable people. They should not go to people who would normally pay to get in. They may be nice guys, but we are nice guys too, and we deserve to have something to show for all of our hard work, even if the money that is earned is not money that goes into our own pockets.

Remind people who want comps that the only income is from ticket sales, that it's only ten or twelve bucks, that if they don't like the show *they can get their money back. One hundred percent guaranteed.* You will always sell more tickets than you will refund. It's difficult to imagine the kind of person who would ask for his or her money back at a small show sponsored by and benefiting a church, but some people will achieve the comfort level necessary to purchase a ticket only when they hear "money-back guarantee." So give it to them.

Think of comps as promotional tickets. When you limit the giving of comps to opening night, you get something in exchange for those tickets: You get people who see the show early and then talk about it to their friends and families. They help start the buzz. Remind people when you give them their free tickets: "Please tell your friends what you liked about the show." Giving comps on closing night makes little sense, unless they are for someone who has a special situation; this is the exception, not the rule.

Miscellaneous matters

When the performance is over and the cast has taken its final bow of the night, have one of the leading actors tell the audience how many performances are left and suggest that they tell their friends about the show and how much they enjoyed it. Say something like "Thanks for coming. We really appreciate your interest. We want to keep doing shows like this, and for that to happen, we need you to tell your friends who may enjoy this to come to the show. All the advertising dollars in the world mean nothing compared to a recommendation from a friend. So if you liked the show, tell your like-minded friends to come. If you hated the show, tell someone you hate to come. Vengeance is sweet. Thanks."

Make sure ushers say "Thank you for coming to the show" to each person in the audience as they leave the building. Have one or two additional people posted at the door for that purpose only. They can also hand out promotional material about the next event, but that is secondary. People will appreciate a chance to thank you right back. The audience wants to clap for you, so let them.

Thoughts about producing out of town

Let's say you've got a motivated cast and a great little show that is so easy to set up that you think you can take it to other churches and other towns. You have some work ahead of you. But with preparation and some help in the town where you are going, it can be done.

The fact that your show has no track record in the out-of-town location is naturally counterbalanced by the fact that the show is an exotic event. You may never be back, or may not be back for a long time. There are people in this town who are tired of the locals and dying to see something novel, and they'll come just to see the out-of-towners while they have the chance.

Ask the host organization or church to do the same marketing you would do, as outlined above. Provide them with your press materials and photos so that they can try to get into the local newspaper. Send them any press clippings (reviews, cast interviews, etc.) that appeared in your own local paper so that the host's local paper can quote from or reprint it. Whoever is coordinating your appearance at the out-of-town location is likely to be someone who enjoys being in the know and likes to spread the news. Give them all the tools you have to do an effective job.

Finally, make sure you charge enough. When you take your show out of town you will inevitably have to pay some of the people something for their time, or you may have to rent a van, or you might even need to spend a night in a motel. If you can't get a deal that pays for expenses such as these and makes sense for the participants, don't go.

START A SPIRIT-BASED THEATER FESTIVAL

Consider: You are producing two or three shows a year in your church. You have found other churches in the area that have theater programs, or there are people in your community working independently to make great work, and you want to showcase it for the community. Let's say there is a synagogue and a Hindu group and some Muslims who have all produced some sort of work like this, and you wish to present an interfaith dialogue on stage to show a mutual respect. Why not create a festival?

What that means is you pool your resources for identifying

and publicizing to an audience, and you produce a weekend where you encourage the patrons of one group to see the shows of the others. Have the shows located in one venue, or if you have too many for that, arrange venues that are within walking distance of each other. Create a ticket deal that encourages people to see more than one show: pay for four and get the fifth one free.

This is a similar system to how fringe festivals operate throughout the world, with a very significant difference: The various sponsoring organizations would need to work together to select a good mix of content. You will most likely want to keep the overall vision of the festival "on topic" (that is, about spiritual issues in general), while at the same time assuring that you have contrasting and even differing viewpoints and perspectives represented. For such a festival to be appealing and successful, the performances will need to have the right mix of commonality and diversity.

Every great festival starts with a great lease. Find a home for the festival in a place that is not depending on you to make a significant payment for rent. Free rent is best, nominal rent is next best. Schedule a Friday-Saturday-Sunday distribution of shows, and make sure every show is performed at least three times so that word-of-mouth has time to build on the good ones. Try to include kid-friendly shows, especially shows that include kids as performers. Having an inexpensive place to take the kids on Saturday afternoon will bring in adults who might otherwise not have considered attending, and if they have a good experience they might just come back for their own benefit later or the next day. Over time, you can add a night to the schedule every year.

Every city has its own rhythms, every audience has its own pace. But a basic festival blueprint along these lines will work in most contexts. And keep in mind that administrative improvisation is essential to the success of any creative venture.

A FINAL NOTE

You are all in this together. The smallest thing—a bit part, a technical effect—can make a show click, or it can bring it to a grinding halt. Everyone, onstage and off, is on the same team and should act accordingly. Patience, pain management, forgiveness, everything we talk about in church, is put to the test in a theatrical endeavor. And it is a great opportunity to prove we have learned something.

8

Some Concluding Remarks

What I have tried to establish in this effort is the validity of a program of church theater and drama ministry. It can take many forms, but the essential elements are explored here. The tradition is as old as theater itself, and its exclusion from the church as a means of education, praxis, outreach, evangelism, and fundraising is an error that can be easily corrected. And the start-up costs can be negligible.

Education

Whatever text or experience you draw from in the creation of a work, you are expanding the world of the participants in the production as well as those in the audience. For this reason alone it is worth the effort as a means of studying a text or a topic with depth and concentration.

Praxis

Engaging congregants, including youth, in meaningful work that deals with significant issues gives them responsibility and a chance to shine. It encourages all members to invite their peers to participate, instead of isolating their church work as a separate compartment away from school, work, hobbies, and other activities.

Outreach

By bringing in people who are not members into the church, word spreads that something interesting is happening, and people arrive at the door of the church for a new encounter with it. This encourages the portal experience of getting people across the threshold instead of allowing them to wander past for years without discovering the life of the congregation within.

Evangelism

Aside from the chance to invite people in, the play is stating some of the core values of faith as a way to articulate what the faith means to them. Those values have to be put in the mouths of amateur actors, so they had better be rendered accessible.

Fundraising

More people will come to a service that features some chancel drama. Beyond a better result in the offering plate, there will evolve a renewed interest in the kind of church that embarks on animating faith stories through live performance. Also, the notion can be fostered that a performance like this can be handled outside the context of the service. An admission fee can be charged to raise money for specific projects. Finally, the ongoing nature of inviting people in to see or hear or participate in the process can become a hallmark of the life of the church.

The separation of church and stage has gone on long enough. Healing the split between the world of theater and the life of congregations offers a rich opportunity for the exchange of insight, literature, and experience. The bonds forged in producing an amateur production as part of church service, educational programming, or as a fundraising endeavor are long lasting and vital. This experiment is the tip of an ice cube on the tip of an iceberg.

Appendix A:
Two Plays by Dean J. Seal

THREE WISE MEN AND ONE WISE GUY: A CHRISTMAS PAGEANT

by Dean J. Seal

Characters

Choir

Christmas Angels

Mary

Joseph

Baby Jesus

Ox

Ass

Camel

Luke

Matthew

Dietrich

Martin

Mohandas

Shepherds

Sheep

Jack Finnegan

Herod

SCENE ONE

(The Choir is singing the Hodie *from "A Ceremony of Carols." The men join in an octave lower on the second time through. They all sing softly.*

Two Angels come in right after the first verse begins, on stilts (preferably), with wings and halos, and they are spreading snow. They are dressed in white, or red and green, with wings, symbolizing Christmas Angels. They are tossing handfuls of snow, or white flower petals, slowly and gracefully.

Behind them immediately are the choir, coming in from the back, in procession, with green crowns and red robes. They are followed by Mary, Joseph, and Baby Jesus, who take their place at the base of the chancel. Following them are Ox, Ass, and Camel, making soft lowing sounds appropriate to their species. They come in a stately stroll. They are followed by Luke and Matthew.

When the choir finishes the Hodie *they are to take positions on both sides of the chancel. As they finish, the Three Wise Men start down the aisle from the back, slowly, so that Luke may begin to narrate.*

Luke the Doctor and Matthew stand at the top step of the chancel, each with a great book. Both look like they are prepared to speak, but Luke gets there first.)

LUKE

Inasmuch as many have taken in hand to set in order a narrative of those things which have been fulfilled, it seemed good to me also, Luke the Physician, having had perfect understanding of all things from the very first, to write to you an orderly account, oh Lover of God, that you may know with certainty the things in which you were instructed.

And it came to pass that in those days, a decree went out from Caesar Augustus that all the world should be counted in a census. So all went, each to his own city. Joseph went out of Nazareth to Bethlehem, because he was of the house of David, to be registered there with Mary, his betrothed wife, who was with child. So it was when they were there the days were completed for her to be delivered. And she brought forth her first born son, and wrapped him swaddling clothes, and laid him in a manger, because there was no room for them at the inn.

SCENE TWO

JOSEPH

(Knocks) Anyone there?

MARY

Urg.

INNKEEPER

We don't want any.

JOSEPH

Please, listen. My wife is great with child. So great, in fact, that if she got any greater, I'd need two donkeys.

INNKEEPER

Sorry, mister. The place is full up. Full. I am great with guests. If I had any more, like you, you'd be sharing a room with someone else who has already paid for it. Try the Comfort Inn down the street.

JOSEPH

Everyone's booked. We've been all over. Give us a break! Can we stay in the laundry room?

INNKEEPER

No. 'fraid not.

MARY

UUUGGGHHH!!!

INNKEEPER

Geez, lady, you are ready to pop.

JOSEPH

What did I tell you?

INNKEEPER

Tell you what. Take your donkey down back to the stable. Stay there. It smells like hay, but I just cleaned it, it's warm, the animals keep it warm, no one will bother you. You'll be off the streets.

JOSEPH

How much?

INNKEEPER

No charge. I'm making plenty tonight. I don't need your money.

JOSEPH

We thank you.

INNKEEPER

Hey. I got an idea. Let the cows and the donkeys eat. Then after she has the kid, the baby can sleep in the manger. I used to do that with my kids when I was down there milking the goats. Used to put 'em down for a nap. Works great. You got swaddle?

JOSEPH

Yes we're all set.

MARY

(*With great urgency*) Joseph, will you get going! Please! *(Mary huffs and puffs.)*

JOSEPH

Okay! Okay! *(They move off to the chancel.)*

INNKEEPER

Good luck! Don't scare the camel!

SCENE THREE

MATTHEW

(Interrupting) Now, the birth of Jesus the Messiah took place in this way, as I, Matthew, have written. In the time of King Herod, wise men from the east came to Jerusalem, asking:

DIETRICH

Where is the child, chosen by God, born King of the Jews?

MARTIN

We have observed his star at its rising. We have come to follow it here.

MOHANDAS

And we have come to pay him homage.

MATTHEW

When King Herod heard this he was frightened.

HEROD

(Aside) Who is this that is born to be king? I have killed my own sons to maintain my throne. And now these magicians are telling me that one is born chosen by God. I must find that child and be done with him.

MATTHEW

Herod learned from his advisors that the Messiah was to be born in Bethlehem, and then he called forth the Wise Men.

(The Wise Men approach Herod.)

HEROD

I am Herod, chosen by Rome, made King of the Jews. See here, go and search diligently for the child, and when you have found him, bring me word so that I may also go and pay him homage.

SCENE FOUR

MATTHEW

They set out, and when they saw the star had stopped over the place where the child was, they were overwhelmed with joy. On entering the house, they saw the child with Mary his Mother, and they knelt down, and they paid him homage. Then, opening their treasure chests, they offered him gifts of gold, frankincense, and myrrh.

DIETRICH

I brought some incense from the Franks, to make the home smell sweet and clean, even though it is a stable for the donkeys. It is a gift for a king.

MARTIN

I brought gold from the south shores of Africa, so that the new mother could begin her days of nurture free of want. It is a gift for a king.

MOHANDAS

I have brought myrrh from India, a sweet resin that will relieve pain for the mother. But it won't be enough. Her joy will turn to bitter sorrow, and her myrrh will change from relieving her pain to embalming her son. It is a gift for the tomb of a king.

MARY

(The Jewish Mom) Thanks, guys, I appreciate it. But if you had been three wise *women,* you would have gotten here before the baby! You would have brought something to eat! You would have brought some clean linens so that I may change the swaddling

clothes! But you are men, and you brought the things that men bring. Money, and luxury items. Did any of you stop and ask directions? I didn't think so. Do me a favor? Run out to the Damascus gate and find us a little pita bread and some lamb. Some cheese would be nice. And see if there is any goat's milk. *(The Wise Men sigh and look embarrassed. They exit.)*

SCENE FIVE

(Shepherds and Sheep assemble before the congregation.)

LUKE

(Speaks while walking from the chancel to the aisle) Now there were in the same country shepherds, living out in the fields, keeping watch over their flocks by night. And behold, an angel of the Lord stood before them, *(an angel comes forward and stands over them)* and the glory of the Lord shone around them, and they were sore afraid.

FIRST SHEPHERD

YOIKS!

SECOND SHEPHERD

JINKIES!

SHEEP

BAAAAAAAAAA!

ANGEL

Do not be afraid, for behold, I bring you good tidings of great joy which will be to all people. For there is born to you this day a savior, the Messiah, the Lord. And this will be a sign to you: you will find the babe wrapped in swaddling clothes and lying in a manger.

LUKE

And suddenly there was with the angel a multitude of the heavenly host, praising God and saying:

ANGELS AND CHOIR

(Stands) Glory to God in the Highest, and on earth Peace, good will to all!

FIRST SHEPHERD

Let us go to Bethlehem and see this thing that has come to pass, which the Lord has made known to us. However, I wish the Lord had made known to us the way to Bethlehem.

LUKE

And they took off in the wrong direction. *(The Shepherds start to head for the back of the sanctuary.)*

SECOND SHEPHERD

I think Bethlehem is this way.

FIRST SHEPHERD

You think so? Should we stop and ask somebody?

SECOND SHEPHERD

I don't want to look like a dummy, let's go this way. We'll find them.

ONE SHEEP

I think that's a BAAAAAAD idea!

FIRST SHEPHERD

Boy, I don't know . . . .

ALL SHEEP

Baaaaa! Baaa! *(They scatter off toward the back of the Sanctuary. They exit.)*

SCENE SIX

(As Shepherds and Sheep leave, The Three Wise Men re-enter with Jack Finnegan and a cohort or two. They are bringing in food and drink for Mary, Joseph, and the Baby. Jack is singing as he enters.)

JACK

(Chorus)

Heyo-Womp-diddy do dah day!

It's time for some goodies, get out of my way!

Yo Ho diddy Ho ho ho! We'll ne'er have enough, and we want
some mo!

Verse One

Oh, Bring me my gifts, let me open some presents

This is not the time now for friendship and sentiment,

Oh fain wouldst thou linger and restrain my finger

from plundering Santa's stocking.

Repeat Chorus (with men from the Choir joining in)

Verse Two

So Hi thee away, bring some pork and some pheasant

This is not the time for the shy or the hesitant

Get out of my path, or you'll taste of my wrath

and a fortnight of pain you'll be clocking

Chorus (with the full Choir joining in)

DIETRICH

Mary, here is the caterer.

JACK

Ho Ho Ha ha hey hey *la dee dah*! Man, do I love Christmas! Boy, do I ever. It's party time! Here's some lamb, and some pita bread, and some goat's milk, and some Swedish meatballs, and some goose, and some turkey, and some pearl onions, . . . man. All the eating, and the presents and the exotic beverages, you know what I'm saying? And the parties! Man, that's what Christmas is all about.

MARY

(A commanding, yet tolerant presence) Excuse me, can you please tell us who you are?

JACK

I'm Jack Finnegan, the hungriest man in town. That's what makes me a good caterer. I'm my own best customer.

DIETRICH

Why are you so happy?

JACK

Cuz it's a birfday party!

MOHANDAS

Whose birthday is it?

JACK

Why, it's . . .it's the *Baby's* birfday. Anyone can see that.

MARTIN

Why are you celebrating this baby's birthday?

JACK

Well because . . . because . . . cuz it's *his Birfday*. It doesn't get any easier than that, pal. And who are you fellas, anyway, dressed so good and lookin' so fine? Yer not from around here, are you?

DIETRICH

No. I have come from Europe to worship this child. My name is Dietrich Bonhoeffer.

JACK

Pleased to meet you, Dieter. Howzabout you?

MARTIN

I have come the long way, from Africa and America, to honor this child. My name is Martin Luther King Junior.

JACK

And you? Skinny Guy?

MOHANDAS

I have come from Asia to praise this child. My name is Mohandas Gandhi. We have come together here, on this spot, in the life of this child.

MARTIN

We actually come from farther away than that. Almost 2000 years farther. We come from the Future.

JACK

The Future? How d'ya do that?

DIETRICH

Don't ask. We have come to honor this child, who has given us so much. He will grow to be a great teacher, a great rabbi, who gives us the key to a new way to live. We bring small gifts to help him survive his childhood.

JACK

Presents? Did you say gifts? Whatja get *me?*

MARTIN

You got the catering gig. Don't complain.

JACK

Awwwww.

MOHANDAS

Please. It's not like we are as rich as three kings.

ALL THREE

HA HA HA HA HA!!!

MARTIN

As the Rabbi said, "It is easier for a camel to get through the eye of a needle than it is for a rich man to enter the Kingdom of God."

MOHANDAS, MARTIN, AND DIETRICH

(The three huddle together, nod and smile their assent.) Good one. Yes. Yes.

JACK

Oh, come on, now, people! We're supposed to love being rich! That's why we're celebrating.

MARTIN

We are celebrating because God sent us his own child to teach us how to live and how to die. This baby will grow up to say, "Love your enemy." Love your enemy! Do you know why? Because love is the most powerful force in the universe. It is the only thing that can change an enemy into a friend.

JACK

Wow.

DIETRICH

Jesus challenged the authority of the powerful. His death was not accidental. He could have stayed in his hometown as a teacher and lived a long life.

MARTIN

As could you, Dieter.

MOHANDAS

As could you, Martin.

DIETRICH

As could you, Mohandas.

MOHANDAS

The call of this child is the call to be ready to give everything, including your life, if that is what it takes, to defeat evil.

JACK

Wait a minute. You guys said it transformed your life. So once you took that big old Jesus pill, everything was okay, right? Didn't that mean it made you rich and successful and powerful and confident? Doesn't it make you sexy and handsome and cute? Make you walk with a bounce in your step? Isn't this like a really good insurance policy?

ALL THREE

Ah, no.

DIETRICH

That's not quite how it works. I was hanged by the Nazis a few days before the end of the Second World War.

MARTIN

I was killed for opposing an unjust war, while I fought for the rights of the garbage men of Memphis.

MOHANDAS

I was struggling for peace between my people the Hindus and our brothers the Muslims, and I was killed by one of my own, for being too accommodating.

DIETRICH

You don't have to be a Jew to be killed by the Nazis.

MARTIN

You don't have to be in Rome to be killed by the Empire.

MOHANDAS

You don't have to be a Christian to die for what Jesus taught.

JACK

Huh! Bet you guys are kicking yourselves now!

ALL THREE

(They face Jack together) I wouldn't change a thing.

MARTIN

Jack. Enjoy this season. Help bring joy to people in the cold and darkness of the winter. You know how to do that.

MOHANDAS

Jack, open your presents with joy and appreciation. Everyone loves being a successful giver.

DIETRICH

Jack, Jesus said, "I give to you a new commandment, that you love one another as I have loved you." Many people lose hope at Christmas. Bring them your joy.

MARTIN

It's not a small thing, Jack. Hospitality is an act of love, and therefore, it is infinite. That joy is sacred, and that joy is in you. Share it.

DIETRICH

Jesus said, "I have come to you that you might live life abundantly." That abundance is the joy of giving.

MOHANDAS

God's heart broke for him, and it breaks for you. Let us celebrate God's goodness and God's love, by celebrating the birth of the son God sent.

(Pause)

JACK

I got a pair of barbecued goats out in the car and a half gallon of raisin sauce. Who's hungry?

EVERYONE

(Cheers) Yeay! *(Then stop. The Shepherds and Sheep enter from stage right.)*

FIRST SHEPHERD

Save some for us! We are so hungry! We made it, and we're starving—LOOK! There's the Baby!

SECOND SHEPHERD

In swaddling clothes! In a manger!

THIRD SHEPHERD

We saw Angels, who told us that the Messiah was born. They said this was not just for the Hebrews, but for everybody.

SECOND SHEPHERD

Good news of great joy to all people. Even us!

MOHANDAS

This is the child you have been searching for.

MARTIN

I had a dream, last night—not that one, another one. I had a dream that an angel came to me and said:

ANGEL

Do not to return to Herod. He would put the child to death in his jealousy and greed. After you have seen and blessed the child, return to your homes.

MARTIN

So let us prepare a meal, and then return to our homelands, Asia, Africa, Europe, and the Americas, to bring this marvelous news.

DIETRICH

Let's all sing a happy song together, and then we'll go break
bread.

MOHANDAS

And let us hope that someone has brought some vegetarian
lasagna.

LUKE AND MATTHEW, ALL ANGELS

And all who heard it marveled at those things that were told them
by the shepherds. But Mary kept all these things, and pondered
them, in her heart.

*(They all smile. The bells sound the opening note for "Joy to the World."
The choir, the shepherds, and sheep gather around the mother and child,
they sing slowly and with awe. When all the verses are done, bells ring
in the tonic of the key of the closing of the "Ceremony of Carols." The
choir sings it as the processional on the way out, male and female voices.
The cast goes out in reverse order. The Angels are last. As they reach the
nave, they softly blow on two ram horns to signal the end.)*

End of Ceremony

HEROD AND PILATE:
A PALM SUNDAY CHANCEL DRAMA

by Dean J. Seal

Herod and Pilate is a work of the imagination that draws from selected biblical texts and the insights brought by modern scholarship to our understanding of the execution of Jesus, especially in terms of traditional teachings that have created virulent anti-Semitism. This is, then, a dramatic and not historic retelling; it is one dramatist's attempt to shed new light on an oft-told tale.

Speaking parts in order of appearance

Mary the Mother

Narrator

Jesus

Caiaphas

Mary Magdalene

Pontius Pilate

Herod Antipas

Mary the Mother

(Speaks from the chancel) His whole family told him not to come here. We told him it is too dangerous for someone like him. He speaks so beautifully, and then he says things that make people want to kill him! He almost was killed by his own people after one speech in the temple! We asked him to come home to his brothers and his mother, and he said, "Those who do the will of God are my brothers and my mother and my sisters." Fat lot of good that will do in Jerusalem. He never thinks of himself. He never thinks of his responsibility to his family. Who will take care of an old woman if he is killed? I will starve to death. Or I'll be made into a slave in someone's household, and if I'm lucky I will be spared. His followers feed me now, because I travel near him, but they will scatter like bees if the Romans take him. Jesus. Why do you do this to your mother who loves you? He'll end up like that John the Baptist.

Narrator

(Speaks from the middle of the sanctuary) Jesus went on ahead, going up to Jerusalem. When he had come to the Mount of Olives, he sent two of his disciples, saying,

Jesus

(Speaks from the back of the sanctuary) Go into the village ahead of you, and as you enter you will find tied there a colt that has never been ridden. Untie it and bring it here. If anyone asks you, "Why are you untying it?" just say this: "The Lord has need of it."

Narrator

So those who were sent departed and found it as he had told them. Then they brought the colt to Jesus, and after throwing their cloaks on the colt, they set Jesus on it. As he rode along, people kept spreading their cloaks on the road. This took place to fulfill what had been spoken through the prophet in Zechariah 9:9, saying, "Tell the daughter of Zion, 'Look, your king is coming to you, humble and mounted on a donkey, on a colt, the foal of a donkey.'"

CONGREGATION

The Great Crowd that had come to the Festival heard Jesus was coming to Jerusalem. So they took branches of palm trees and went out to meet him, shouting.

NARRATOR

(Walks in front of Jesus down the aisle) As he was now approaching the path down from the Mount of Olives, the whole multitude of the disciples began to praise God joyfully with a loud voice for all the deeds of power that they had seen, saying:

CONGREGATION

Hosanna! Save us! Hosanna to the Son of David! Blessed is the king who comes in the name of the Lord! Blessed is the one who comes in the name of the Lord, the King of Israel! Peace in Heaven, and glory in the highest heaven! Save us! Hosanna! Save us!

NARRATOR

So then the crowd that had been with him when he called Lazarus out from the tomb and raised him from the dead continued to testify. It was also because they had heard he had performed this sign that the crowd went to meet him. The Pharisees then said to one another:

CAIAPHAS

(At center of chancel) You see, we can do nothing. Look, the world has gone after him! Many Jews are deserting us because they have seen Lazarus raised from the dead. My scribes come to me and say, "If we let him go on like this, everyone will believe in him and the Romans will come and destroy both our holy place and our nation." I say to them, "You know nothing at all! You do not understand that it is better for you to have one man die for the people than to have the whole nation destroyed."

When Babylon destroyed the Temple and we were in Exile for seventy years, it almost destroyed Israel as a people. The Romans are much stronger. When they destroyed Carthage, they killed every man, violated every woman and sold every child into slavery. They pulled down its great buildings, and they sowed the earth with salt so that nothing would ever prosper there again. I tell you, it will happen to us if this Jesus cannot be stopped.

Put out the word. The Romans want to arrest him, and we will help. Jesus has not been in plain view for weeks until this conspicuous, contemptuous mockery of the entry into Jerusalem of the Proconsul. This demonstration of contempt will not go unnoticed by Pilate, and he will turn his wrath on us. Pilate is a great believer in killing people. He crucified two thousand Pharisees just a few years ago. Pilate is ready to kill, and my people are ready to die. If Jesus does one more thing to insult us in our authority over the people or to the Romans, it could be the end of everything. *(Caiaphas retires)*

CONGREGATION

Then Jesus entered the temple and drove out all who were selling and buying in the temple, and he overturned the tables of the Money changers and the seats of those who sold doves. He said to them:

JESUS

(From the floor in front of the chancel) It is written, "My house will be a house of Prayer!" But you have made it a den of robbers! *(Scatters coins, turns over table)*

MARY MAGDALENE

I have followed him for a long time now, feeding him and his disciples from my substance, keeping clothes on their backs and finding them a place for the night when he was ready to sleep outside again. Outside! I have seen him heal, and I have even seen him raise the dead. He has said so many beautiful things, but he also asks the impossible. Turn the other cheek so they can strike you again. Forgive all debts. Lend money to people who can't pay you back. Give money to anyone who asks. Does he understand how many times you can be asked?

Now he comes to Jerusalem. He cannot hide here, like he did in the countryside when Herod Antipas was looking for him. Now he's going to . . . what? Teach the Romans in the Temple? Convert the Sadducees to his cause? His kingdom is everywhere, he says, but it won't defend him if he's attacked. Where does he think he lives? This is no Garden of Eden here. This is modern civilization! The Romans have a sword to your throat, and we better produce results, or blood will flow. If we turn the other cheek to the Romans, they will separate our heads from our necks. We can't turn the other neck.

Now he comes to Jerusalem. He's just asking to be killed.

(She exits left. Pilate and Caiaphas enter from the right, pacing slowly with their arms behind their backs.)

PILATE

Caiaphas, I hate coming to Jerusalem every year, but every year the city seems ready to explode. You people need to understand that the Roman Empire has given you a great service in allowing your temple to be rebuilt. People come from all over the empire to worship at it and marvel at its beauty.

CAIAPHAS

They are strangers to our God, and come with no interest in learning about El Shaddai. They come to be pious in an ignorant way, to make sacrifices to hedge their bets, and then they go off to worship in another city, to another god, at another temple.

PILATE

Yet they leave behind a great deal of money. That is why your late king Herod the Great built up your courtyard of the Gentiles. That is why Herod the Great built up the Port at Caesarea. The income from these pious travelers would refill your temple treasury many times over.

CAIAPHAS

Those donations are to the Glory of God, and are distributed to the poor.

PILATE

(Angry) Yet this Nazarene comes in and throws them all out! That's not very hospitable! And your people cheer him for it! He begins teaching in the temple and they flock to hear him!

Who is in charge of the temple, here, Caiaphas? You or Yeshua? He hasn't been in town for more than a few days and everyone is ready to rise up behind him. His swarm of followers from the countryside is infecting the whole city.

CAIAPHAS

We cannot arrest him in the temple. His teachings have not given us cause to arrest him. We have tried to trap him with problems from the Torah, yet he manages an answer that allows him to escape every time. He's too clever.

PILATE

You need an excuse to arrest him?

CAIAPHAS

We cannot just arrest him during the festival, or there may be a riot among the people.

PILATE

Can't you arrest him where he lives? Catch him by stealth, when he is asleep. At midnight, even the King of the Jews must sleep!

CAIAPHAS

You cannot make light of that! We do not know where he sleeps! He looks like he sleeps outside, in the dirt. That is his habit. He is as wild as John the Baptist.

PILATE

We need to kill him the way Herod killed the Baptist. That was the end of the Baptist movement. Let me make this clear. You find where he sleeps, and bring my men there, and we will arrest him and deal with him. And it has to be before the Sabbath and Passover celebrations, or the whole town will break open, and neither you nor I can prevent the bloodshed. But both of us will pay with our lives if this city breaks open again.

CAIAPHAS

I may know a way.

PILATE

If you fail, your nation will be rubbed off the face of the earth. Your temple will be famous as a lost treasure, like the Colossus at Rhodes. The Jews will go down as an unlucky people that claimed the center of the busiest highway in the history of humanity. Do not fail, Caiaphas.

(Exit)

JESUS

(Off to the side) Abba, if it is possible, let this cup pass from me. Yet not what I want, but whatever you want. *(Guards enter. Turns, says angrily)* Have you come out with swords and clubs to arrest me, as though I were a bandit? Day after day I sat in the temple teaching, and you did not lay hands on me. But This Is Your Hour, and the Hour of the Power of Darkness!

HYMN

(At this point the play pauses and the choir and congregation sing a hymn such as, from the Presbyterian hymnal, no. 83, "Oh Love How Deep (Agincourt)," no. 85, "What Wondrous Love," no. 93, "Ah, Holy Jesus," or no. 365, "Jesus Priceless Treasure." The cast does not sing; they remain in character but at rest.)

(Caiaphas and Jesus enter to left center floor)

CAIAPHAS

If you are the Messiah, tell us.

JESUS

If I tell you, you will not believe. If I question you, you will not answer. But from now on, The Son of Man will be seated at the right hand of the power of God.

CAIAPHAS

Are you then, the son of God?

JESUS

You say that I am.

CAIAPHAS

Let us bring him before Pilate.

(They go up the chancel to Pilate) We have found this man perverting our nation. He stirs up the people by teaching throughout all of Judea, from Galilee where he began, even unto Jerusalem.

PILATE

Are you as they say? Are you saying you are the king of the Jews?

JESUS

You say so.

PILATE

You hear the accusations they make against you? *(Silence)* That's not much of a defense. He's from Galilee? Then I am sending you to Herod Antipas to be judged. You should have better answers than that when you speak to Herod. If Herod thinks you are no threat to your people, I will set you free. But if Herod Antipas finds you to be another Baptist, you will go the way of the Baptist. He could clip your head off like an errant toenail. If you come back to me, I will not be as kind to you as Herod was to the Baptizer.

Let us send him to Herod. He is in town for the festival; let him bear the burden of this man's judgment. If Jesus is to be killed, I don't want the Romans to be blamed. We have enough trouble with this festival. Every year you celebrate your freedom from the Egyptians, and you look at your service to Rome with angry eyes. Remember, we protect you from the Parthians. They may not be as generous about you worshiping your God as we are. We honor the Antiquity of your God, and allow you the pleasure of worshiping at your holy place. But all that comes to an end if your Nazarene comes into the City to disrupt the respectful tribute of the citizens of Rome. Tell Herod what is at stake here. See if there is a way to keep this Jesus in close quarters in Galilee. If he can be persuaded to stay in his hometown, he will be allowed to teach whatever he wants.

CAIAPHAS

No! His teachings must be stopped! All worship is to take place in Jerusalem! All teaching must come from the temple scribes!

PILATE

Do not the Samaritans read your same five holy books of Moses?
Yet they worship in the high places, and burn sacrifices on the
hilltops. They are compliant to the Romans. So are the Galileans
under Herod. *(To Jesus)* If Herod Antipas can overlook this temple outrage, and keep you in his district, you may live. I suggest
to you, if you are to be King of the Jews, be King of the Jews of
Galilee, and share your kingship with Herod Antipas. He could
be a very good friend to you.

JESUS

That fox was a very good friend to John the Baptist.

(Pilate and Caiaphas exit. Herod enters)

HEROD

So Jesus of Nazareth, son of Mary, rabbi of Capernaum. Last I
heard from you, you sent me word that you were to be killed in
Jerusalem. Remember? "Listen! I must be on my way because it
is impossible for a prophet to be killed out of Jerusalem." Remember saying that? Looks like you may have your chance. All
I ever wanted to do was see you. Talk with you. See the miracle
worker. I got to know John very well. He was the holy man you
followed, wasn't he? You were baptized with the rest of them,
weren't you? *(Silence)* I know you were shocked at his sudden
death. So was I. John was not sane. He angered my wife against
me. Who can do that to a tetrarch and escape punishment? I
protected him as long as I could. My wife would have had him
dead long before he was actually killed. I loved to listen to him
talk about things. Amazing things. Are you as amazing as he?
I've been wanting to hear you speak for a long time now. *(Silence)* Can I tell you something? This conversation is your last

chance. Calling yourself the King of the Jews is stupider than making my wife angry. You're making a Roman Governor angry. And he's a killer. You knew that when you went to Jerusalem. You couldn't miss the Pharisees that are still rotting away on their crosses.

Listen. I'm alive because I'm not stupid. You and I can make an agreement. You go back to your lovely home in Capernaum. I'll get the roof fixed. You stay there and teach, do that healing thing everyone is talking about, forget this King of the Jews thing. We'll have more people crowding into Galilee than those Sadducee idiots have down at the temple. We can both do really well. You can heal and preach. I'll make sure you have protection, as long as you don't leave town. Think of how many you can save. What could be wrong with that? *(Silence)* Or, I can tell Pilate that you are a dangerous heretic, determined to become king, and have you whipped and sent back for a slow death on a Roman cross. *(Pause)* Decide. *(Pause)* Now. *(Silence. Herod sighs.)* Guard! Take this prisoner and beat him. Then, put him in my best purple robe. Shape a crown for this king from the thorns of my wife's rose bush, and jam it onto his head. Send him back to Pilate. I can't afford to kill another baptizer. Tell Pilate that this is a rebellious political enemy of Rome, and he should be executed in the customary way without delay. But recommend to him that he start in the morning, so it is happening before the crowds are awake.

(Herod exits. Pilate and Caiaphas re-enter and approach Jesus)

PILATE

So, Your highness. You have returned from Herod. He has not saved you. Are you the King of the Jews?

JESUS

Do you ask this on your own, or did others tell you about me?

PILATE

I am not a Jew, yet your own nation and chief priests have handed you over to me. For the last time. What have you done?

JESUS

My kingdom is not of this world. If it were, my followers would be fighting to keep me from being handed over. But as it is, my kingdom is not from here.

PILATE

So you are a king?

JESUS

You say that I am king. For this I was born, and for this I came into the world, to *testify to the truth.* Everyone who belongs to the truth listens to my voice.

PILATE

What is truth? . . . Truth to you and your dirty little tribe is that this is your God's land, and he has given it to you to care for. Look around you. Any idiot can see it is Roman land now. From Gaul to Golgotha. Your God seems to lose again and again. You may be king of your truth, whatever it is, but your truth will die with you, like baptism died with John.

JESUS

My kingdom is free of kings. My disciples will cure the sick and will eat with the destitute. My kingdom shall have no end.

PILATE

A kingdom with no kings, where the soldiers share their food with the starving. Huh. Every kingdom has its end when it comes into contact with Rome. I'll show you what we do with kings. Guard! Crucify this man when the sun comes up. And wait. Above his head you must post a sign, have it written in Latin, Greek, and Hebrew. It should read thusly, "Jesus the Nazarene, king of the Jews."

CAIAPHAS

Do not write that, but write "This man *said* he was king of the Jews."

PILATE

What I have written, I have written.

(They all exit. The two Marys enter.)

MARY MAGDALENE

His time has come, and we are left with, what? Some memories of what he said? Who knows all of them? He said so many things. We thought he would sit down and tell them to a scribe some day, like a prophet, but he never sat still long enough. Now we'll have to piece it together, if we remember anything at all.

MARY MOTHER

This is what he did. He shared his food. He washed our feet. He did not fear death. He brought us the kingdom of God, which is all around us. He gave us to know the presence of God, the Holy Spirit of God, to come to us and permeate us with his goodness, his love and his mercy. In his face, he showed us the soul of our God. And for this, he would have to die. Such a waste.

MARY MAGDALENE

John the Baptizer's light went out when he was executed. Only a few of his followers remain. But Jesus sent his disciples out, each to heal, to do what he did. Those bumbling, idiotic disciples that Jesus spent so much time yelling at, now it is up to them. I hope God does not abandon them. The way he abandoned Jesus.

NARRATOR

Let us read together.

CONGREGATION

So they took Jesus, and carrying the cross by himself, he went out to what is called The Place of the Skull, which in Hebrew is called Golgotha. There they crucified him, and with him two others, one on each side, with Jesus in between them. And the soldiers who had crucified him took his clothes and divided them.

The End

Appendix B: Works Cited and Additional Resources

WORKS CITED

Erskine, Noel Leo. *King Among the Theologians.* Cleveland: Pilgrim Press, 1994.

Kavanaugh, Aidan. *Elements of Rite.* New York: Pueblo Publishing, 1982.

Yates, Wilson. "Intersections of Art and Religion." *Arts Magazine,* 2000, no. 1, 17–27.

ADDITIONAL READING

General Theater, Spirituality, and Theology

Ball, David. *Backwards and Forwards: A Technical Manual for Reading Plays.* Carbondale: Southern Illinois University Press, 1983.

Brook, Peter. *The Empty Space.* New York: Avon Books, 1968.

Brueggemann, Walter. *The Prophetic Imagination.* Second Edition. Minneapolis: Fortress Press, 2001.

Egri, Lahos. *The Art of Dramatic Writing.* New York: Simon and Schuster, 1960.

Heart of the Beast Puppet Theater. *Puppet Cookbook,* Second Edition. They've been making giant and small puppet shows for 25 years, from six inches to 20 feet, and they put all their puppet-making knowledge into this text. Available only from their web site: www.hobt.org.

Seyler, Athene. *The Craft of Comedy: An Exchange of Letters on Comedy Acting Techniques with Stephen Haggard.* New York: Routledge, 1990.

Church and Drama

Corbitt, J. Nathan and Vivian Nix-Early. *Taking It to the Streets: Using the Arts to Transform your Community.* Grand Rapids, MI: Baker Books, 2003.

Custer, Jim and Bob Hoose. *The Best of the Jeremiah People: Humorous Sketches and Performance Tips from America's Leading Christian Repertory Group.* Colorado Springs, CO: Meriwether, 1991.

Drane, Olive M. Fleming. *Clowns, Storytellers, Disciples: Spirituality and Creativity for Today's Church.* Minneapolis: Augsburg Books, 2004.

Pederson, Steve. *Drama Ministry: Practical Help for Making Drama a Vital Part of Your Church.* Grand Rapids, MI: Zondervan, 1999. Includes DVD.

Pitzele, Peter A. *Scripture Windows: Toward a Practice of Bibliodrama.* Los Angeles: Alef Design Group, 1997.

Swanson, Richard. *Provoking the Gospel: Methods to Embody Biblical Storytelling through Drama.* Cleveland: Pilgrim Press, 2004.

Kids

Bernardi, Philip. *Improvisation Starters: A Collection of 900 Improvisation Situations for the Theater.* White Hall, VA: Betterway Publications, 1992.

Muir, Kerry. *Childsplay: A Collection of Scenes and Monologues for Children.* New York: Limelight Editions, 1995.

Novelly, Maria C. *Theater Games for Young Performers: Improvisations and Exercises for Developing Acting Skills.* Colorado Springs, CO: Meriwether, 1985.

Peterson, Lenka and Dan O'Connor. *Kids Take the Stage: Helping Young People Discover the Creative Outlet of the Theater.* New York: Back Stage Books, 1997.

Film and Television

Aichele, George and Richard Walsh. *Screening Scripture: Intertextual Connections between Scripture and Film.* Harrisburg, PA: Trinity Press International, 2002.

Anderson, Philip Longfellow. *The Gospel in Disney: Christian Values in the Early Animated Classics.* Minneapolis: Augsburg Books, 2004.

Anker, Roy M. *Catching Light: Looking for God in the Movies.* Grand Rapids, MI: William B. Eerdmans, 2004.

Barsotti, Catherine and Robert K. Johnston. *Finding God in the Movies: 33 Films of Reel Faith.* Grand Rapids, MI: Baker Books, 2004.

Dark, David. *Everyday Apocalypse: The Sacred Revealed in Radiohead, the Simpsons, and Other Pop Culture Icons.* Grand Rapids, MI: Brazos Press, 2002.

Detweiler, Craig. *A Matrix of Meanings: Finding God in Pop Culture.* Grand Rapids, MI: Baker Academic, 2003.

Jewett, Robert. *Saint Paul at the Movies: The Apostle's Dialogue with American Culture.* Louisville, KY: Westminster/John Knox Press, 1993.

————*Saint Paul Returns to the Movies: Triumph Over Shame.* Grand Rapids, MI: William B. Eerdmans, 1999.

Johnston, Robert K. *Reel Spirituality: Theology and Film in Dialogue.* Grand Rapids, MI: Baker Books, 2000.

Maltin, Leonard. *Leonard Maltin's Family Film Guide.* New York: Signet, 1999.

Pinsky, Mark I. *The Gospel According to the Simpsons: The Spiritual*

Life of the World's Most Animated Family. Louisville, KY: Westminster/John Knox Press, 2001.

Reinhartz, Adele. *Scripture on the Silver Screen.* Louisville, KY: Westminster/John Knox Press, 2003.

Walsh, Richard. *Reading the Gospels in the Dark: Portrayals of Jesus in Film.* Harrisburg, PA: Trinity Press International, 2003.

Organizations

Christians in the Theater Arts. A national organization of networking and skill-sharing. The visible presence of Regents University and Pat Robertson in their materials may be off-putting for some, but still worth checking out. CITA, Box 26471, Greenville, SC 29616; www.cita.org

Minnesota Fringe Festival. The largest non-juried festival in the nation is tied to dozens of fringe festivals all over the world, from the birthplace of fringes in Edinburgh, Scotland, to a couple of dozen in Canada to fringes in Hong Kong and Australia. The Minnesota Fringe Festival is a great resource for ideas about inexpensive theater production, touring a show, and getting connected with great talents. Minnesota Fringe Festival, 528 Hennepin Avenue #503, Minneapolis, MN 55403 (612) 872-1212; www.fringefestival.org

United Theological Seminary. A masters degree program is offered in *Theology and the Arts* (MATA), which deals with the theology and role of painting, sculpture, music, performance, fabric, and other art forms utilized to convey the Spirit to the congregants. This specialty is available along with a program that includes the Master of Divinity, a Master in Religious Leadership, and more; www.unitedseminary-mn.org.